# INDIANAPOLIS Motor Speedway

## 100 Years of Racing

Ralph Kramer

Published by

**700 East State Street • Iola, WI 54990-0001**
**715-445-2214 • 888-457-2873**
**www.krausebooks.com**

Our toll-free number to place an order or obtain
a free catalog is (800) 258-0929.

**Unless otherwise noted, the photographs in this book are courtesy of the Indianapolis Motor Speedway archives.**

Cover photograph courtesy of Indianapolis Motor Speedway archives.

Library of Congress Control Number: 2008937710

ISBN-13: 978-0-89689-835-6
ISBN-10: 0-89689-835-0

Designed by Paul Birling
Edited by Kristine Manty

Printed in China

# ACKNOWLEDGMENTS

To state the obvious, this is a picture book, not a history book. There's only one historian at the Indianapolis Motor Speedway and that's Donald Davidson, whose recall of events and circumstances at the racing capital of the world is legendary. I am immensely grateful for his assistance.

You will find many photos and illustrations here in print for the first time. For that I thank Ron McQueeney's IMS photo department and Ellen Bireley at the Hall of Fame Museum. Special thanks to Mary Ellen Loskar, Jim Haines, Shawn Payne, Dave Hilberry, Sherry Rawson-Koker, Bill Spoerle, A.J. Fairbairn, Dave Harrison, Mary Geiss, Mark Schneider and the museum staff.

Thanks, also, to Speedway executives Joie Chitwood, Peggy Swalls, Kevin Forbes and Fred Nation, as well as Dan Skiver's licensing group.

Many Speedway aficionados contributed to this effort, but none more so than an old *Indianapolis News* colleague, Richard Mittman.

I'm also grateful to Spencer Riggs, Joe Young, Susan Sutton, John Otte, Robert Cassaday, Bob Haag, Don Bailey, Dollie Cole, Pat Cronin, Jim Rathmann, Irene Smith, Leo Mehl, John Cooper, Jack Martin, Scott Harris, Dr. Harlen Hunter, John Gunnell, Tom Kanegy and Chris Economaki, along with the wonderful people at the public libraries in Indianapolis, Speedway, Shelbyville, Greensburg and Terre Haute.

Like the millions who have been affected by the Speedway to one degree or another over the years, I reserve my most heartfelt thank you for Mari, Tony and all the members of the Hulman/George family. If it weren't for their stewardship, there would be no Speedway today. And no 100th birthday to celebrate.

# CONTENTS

# Celebrating 100 Years at the Brickyard

One of the nice things about anniversaries is the opportunity they present for reflection. For the Speedway family, this 100th anniversary has us doing exactly that. We're looking to the future. But we're also looking back beyond the moment when the Hulman-George stewardship began in 1945 all the way to the very beginning.

Knowing what it takes today to accommodate the competitors and the crowds at one of our events, I can't imagine how Carl Fisher's team managed that first race day in 1909. Even if it was a balloon race.

Once the founders got things sorted out, the Speedway's traditional association with world-class championships and world-class events has been its hallmark.

Wilbur Shaw was searching for someone to build on that tradition when he persuaded my grandfather to buy the place almost 65 years ago. In Tony Hulman he found a kindred spirit. He stated it very simply: "I don't care whether I make any money out of it. I'd like to be sure of sufficient income so we could make a few improvements each year and build the Speedway into something everyone could be really proud of."

Those are the words we live by.

Would my grandfather approve of what we've done in the last few years to enhance the facility and expand our activities? I think so. He would certainly agree that we must always give both competitors and spectators at the Speedway a world-class experience they can't get anywhere else. As prudent as he was, he would also respect the idea that the cost of those improvements might best be spread across more than one major event a year.

We began talking to Formula One officials in the early '90s, even before we considered a NASCAR race. We found with the Allstate 400 at the Brickyard and then with the United States Grand Prix that we could manage three huge events a year.

We welcomed the addition of the Red Bull Indianapolis GP to our schedule in 2008. MotoGP promises to offer excitement to new fans as we deliver another world-class event. The return of Formula One in the future would give us an ideal calendar.

With the exception of the Indy 500, which I guarantee will always happen in May and on the oval, I can't say for certain what the Speedway calendar will look like in the years ahead.

But this I can say: Millions and millions of people have passed through our gates in the last 100 years, and no one ever forgot the experience. As much as the place may change in the next 100 years, that part won't. It will always leave a lasting impression.

The Indianapolis Motor Speedway is one very special institution. The Hulman-George family intends to keep it that way.

Tony George
CEO, Indianapolis Motor Speedway

**Tony George.**

# Speedway A Monumental Shrine to Motorsports

## By Mario Andretti

I first heard of Indianapolis around 1950 when I was a kid growing up in Italy. In those days, motor racing was more popular than any other sport in Italy. And my idols were Alberto Ascari and Juan Fangio. But the only time I got a glimpse of Indianapolis was when I went to the movies. During intermission they would show newsreels of major sporting events from around the world and that's where I would see clips of the Indianapolis 500. I told myself: I'm going there someday.

We moved to America in 1955 and the first time I actually set foot on Indianapolis Motor Speedway soil was in 1958 when my brother and I went to watch the race with my Uncle Louie. I was 18 and I felt overcome with excitement and anticipation. As I looked down from our seats at the exit of turn 4, all I could see was a blur. But it was enough. I could imagine the rest—Jimmy Bryan striding down pit lane or Rodger Ward pacing thoughtfully in his garage. When I got home I thought about nothing else for days. In fact, for decades. In fact, I'm still thinking about Indianapolis.

I guess it's pretty clear: I love that place. Now that might seem odd to some since I raced there 29 times from 1965 to 1994 and only won once. I actually had terrible luck. I could go fastest in practice and qualifying and yet during the race, I had my share of problems. If it was a 400-mile race, I definitely would have won more. But here's the thing...every driver still loves Indy, regardless. We love the battle of man and machine to the finish. And we respect the

historical significance of the Speedway. It's not only a shrine of monumental importance to our sport…in Indianapolis, racing is religion. The Speedway is our temple. That's the best way I can explain my worship for Indianapolis.

Besides pure joy, there were two things that track gave me. One was a kind of insecurity, because tragedy sort of lurks in the shadows and it could be all over tomorrow. Especially decades ago when safety wasn't all that important. And more recently watching my two sons, my nephew and my grandson race there. On the other hand, when I won in 1969 it was the most exhilarating experience. Fame came suddenly—a thunderclap, a bolt from the blue. Indianapolis changed my life. Just like that.

I feel spoiled that I got to race 29 times at the Indianapolis Motor Speedway, and that the fans for some reason treated me and the other drivers like kings. I just can't thank them enough. To be treated so well by the people even after retiring from the sport is something I can't explain.

It's always fun to look at old pictures. And looking at the photos in this book should be a nostalgic experience for those who love Indy. I am proud to have had a part in the Speedway for as long as I have. This sentiment is shared by my colleagues and my family. Whatever the changes from one era to the next, the Indianapolis Motor Speedway maintains its character and significance. This wonderful National Historic Landmark symbolizes the continuity of our sport from generation to generation.

**Photos, from top left: Mario's Vel's-Parnelli/Offy, shown here after qualifying, was sidelined with a burned piston on Lap 4 in 1973; Mario with son, Jeff, and grandson, Marco; Juan Manuel Fangio, five-time Grand Prix World Champion.**

Barney Oldfield at the wheel of his Premier racer.

CHAPTER 1

# WILD DREAMS, WILDER DEEDS

One of the few images of Carl Fisher has him in this scholarly pose in 1912.

As the 20th Century dawned, nothing about a piece of the old Pressley farm, a good half-hour's buggy ride west of downtown Indianapolis, suggested the property would soon be world renowned. Or that 100 years later, its greatness had not merely endured, but had been magnified many times over.

The Indianapolis Motor Speedway, a rectangular ribbon of fresh hard-pack with a splendid covered grandstand and a few other buildings down near the southwestern corner, had sprouted like a colossal spring flower in 1909 on a half-section that was cropland and pasture just the year before. The ground was low and wet and a creek ran through it, but it was flat and touched a railroad line, and to its new owners, that made all the difference.

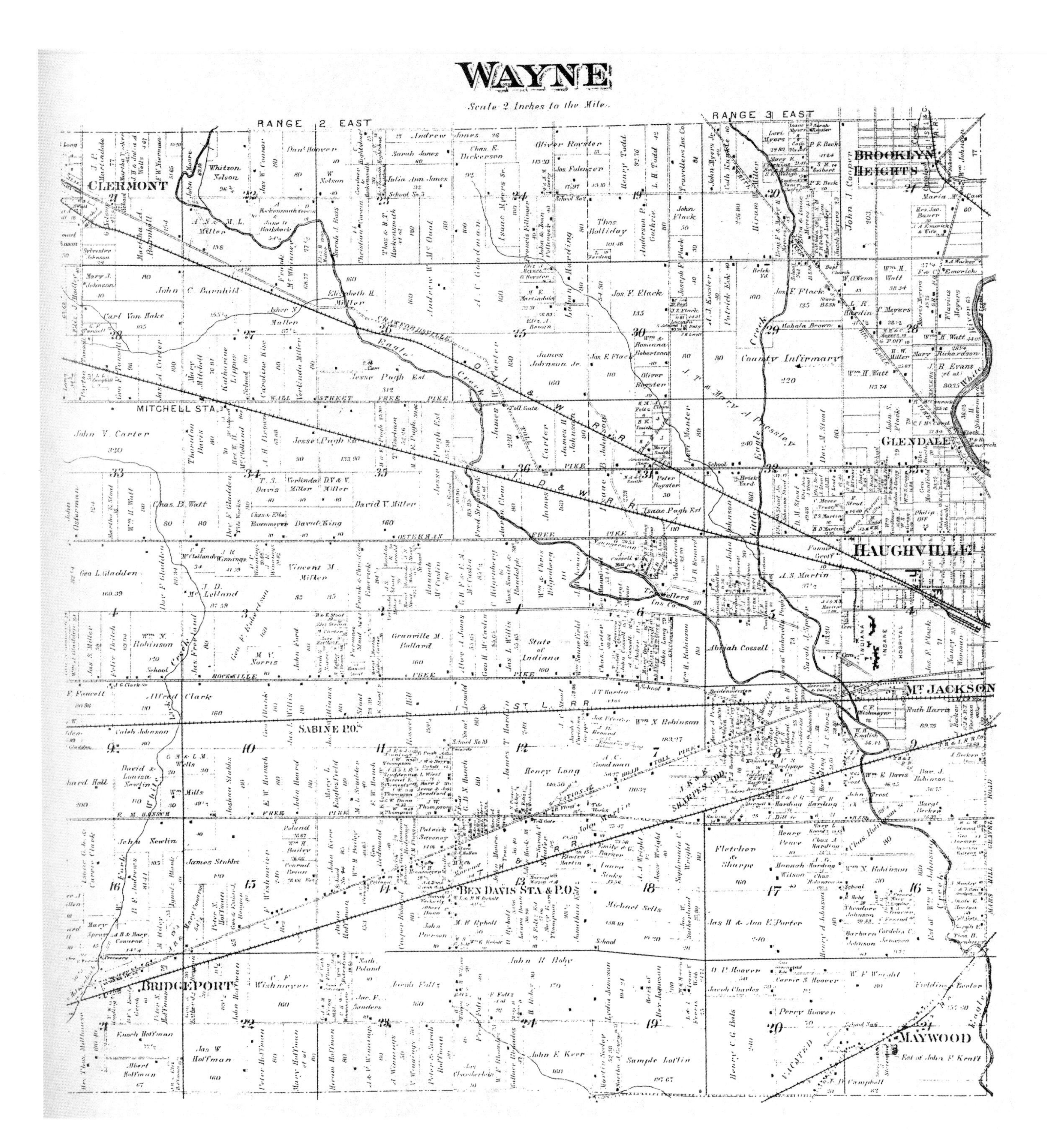

WAYNE
Scale 2 Inches to the Mile.
RANGE 2 EAST
RANGE 3 EAST
CLERMONT
BROOKLYN HEIGHTS
MITCHELL STA.
County Infirmary
GLENDALE
HAUGHVILLE
INDIANA INSANE HOSPITAL
MT JACKSON
SABINE P.O.
BEN DAVIS STA & P.O.
BRIDGEPORT
MAYWOOD

**The four founders of the Speedway: Arthur Newby, Frank Wheeler, Carl Fisher and James Allison.**

At least 50 car companies call Indy home in the early 1900s. As late as 1920, they're still building 100,000 cars a year. But with its focus on more expensive custom vehicles at a time when Detroit is cranking out low-priced versions for the masses, Indy's car capital days are numbered.

The sale price—$300 an acre for 80 acres, $200 for the remaining 240—might bring to mind the old saw about the country bumpkin seeing the city slicker coming. In 2009 dollars, $300 would be about $6,000—big money for marginal Indiana farmland. But it didn't matter to Carl Fisher.

Carl Graham Fisher, 35—"Crazy Carl," they called him—was the driving force in a four-man partnership formed to buy the land and develop the track. The Indianapolis Motor Speedway Company was officially incorporated March 20, 1909, and capitalized at $250,000.

**A 1900s plat map, Wayne Township.** *Indiana Historical Society*

Legal papers listed Arthur C. Newby as first vice-president, Frank H. Wheeler as second vice-president and James A. Allison as secretary-treasurer. Fisher was the president, which was fitting since this was his baby; or more correctly, his latest most stupefying adventure.

A peripatetic street-smart grade-school dropout with bad eyes and a daredevil streak, Carl was P.T. Barnum reincarnated. Born poor in Greensburg, Indiana, on January 12, 1874, he quit school at 12 and got a job in a grocery store to help his mother pay the bills. For awhile, he rode the passenger trains around the Midwest, hawking sundry snacks, reading material and the like. At 17, he

In 1904 Carl Fisher decides to enter the inaugural 1905 Vanderbilt Cup races on Long Island, but he needs a car. He commissions the Premier factory in Indianapolis to build him one. It is a raw machine – not much more than a ladder frame with a pair of primitive seats at the tail and a monster 900-cid four-cylinder air-cooled engine up front. Huge pistons are seven inches across. When Fisher obtains a rulebook, he discovers the car is 300 pounds too heavy. So he okays drilling 256 holes in the frame and 28 more in the rear axle. Still overweight, the car is parked until an outing at the Indiana State Fairgrounds in 1905, which Fisher wins at a tick less than 60 miles an hour. Fisher is photographed here exercising the car at the Speedway around 1915.

One of Carl Fisher's many enterprises in the early 1890s is a riding academy adjacent to his bike store. Attracted by the opportunity to learn the intricacies of the newfangled "safety" cycle from a famous bike racer, kids from the city's finest families are among his students in 1894.

put $600 he had saved into a bicycle repair shop in Indianapolis.

Although Carl was an expert high-wheel rider, the market was being overrun by so-called "safety bikes," with both wheels the same size. Indianapolis residents joined the rest of the country in a veritable bicycle craze. Everybody had to have one.

Soon, bike racing on steep board tracks became all the rage. Many towns had their own teams. Rivalries were intense. Ever the competitor, Fisher was among the best. He and his good friend, Berna Eli "Barney" Oldfield, barnstormed the Midwest as members of Art Newby's Zig-Zag Cycling Club. And yes, it's the same Newby who threw in with Fisher to buy the Pressley farm.

In the years ahead, many of the friends Fisher made as a teen-ager, people like Oldfield, Newby, Jim Allison and Louis Chevrolet, would find their lives inextricably connected in one way or another to the mighty institution that would soon take shape on Indy's far west side.

But not just yet. In 1893, Fisher was doing okay financially repairing and racing bikes, but he knew there was even better money selling them. So, he borrowed train fare and paid visits to bike manufacturers in Ohio.

He hit pay dirt in Toledo, where he charmed Col. Albert Pope into shipping him a carload of bikes at factory cost, and in Columbus, where he persuaded George Erland to not only consign bikes but to finance a dazzling bicycle superstore in downtown Indianapolis.

Back home, he ordered 1,000 small balloons, had a personal note inserted into 50 of them informing the finder that it could be exchanged for a free bicycle, and released them all to soar over the rooftops and church steeples of Indianapolis.

Full-page newspaper ads ignited a frenzy. In her book, *Fabulous Hoosier,* Carl's future wife, Jane, tells the story of men and boys taking up arms and firing away at the balloons as they floated along.

The promotion was a smash hit. It sold more than enough bikes to pay for the giveaways. It put the Fisher store on the map and added to the Fisher reputation for flamboyant merchandising stunts. But the city hadn't witnessed anything yet.

The automobile arrived on the Indy scene in 1898, and there was Carl Fisher in the driver's seat. Although historians argue whether the little $650 de Dion motor tricycle he imported from France was a bona fide automobile, it's generally agreed to be either the first or the second self-propelled four-wheeler ever to ply Indianapolis thoroughfares.

Almost overnight, Fisher abandoned the bicycle business. The bike freak became a car guy.

A trip to the first New York Auto Show in 1900 got him connected with Ransom E. Olds, who was trolling for dealers to sell his cute little curved dash Oldsmobile. Fisher signed up. If he wasn't America's first car dealer, he was close.

Pretty soon, he had a Winton race car, with which he thrilled county fairgoers across the Midwest by racing it against "any horse you want to run against me." The horse always led at the start and Fisher always led at the wire. And afterward, Carl would charge $10 apiece for rides around the track. His first year he cleared $20,000.

By the next summer, fairgoers were paying to watch Fisher, Oldfield, Chevrolet and other old bike racing buddies race each other in their cars. It was great theater. Thousands and thousands came to see the action and went away bitten by the car bug. Everyone wanted to own an automobile and Carl had plenty to sell.

At his ever-larger downtown Indianapolis store, business was brisk. Among the brands he sold was Stoddard-Dayton, which was the star of at least two brilliantly executed Fisher marketing stunts.

One day in 1907, after a lavish publicity build-up, he shoved an S-D off the edge of the roof on a seven-story downtown building. While gawkers gasped, the car crashed to the street and landed on its wheels. Fisher's brothers, Rollo and Earle, were there waiting. One jumped into the driver's seat, the other cranked the engine.

Newspapers reported the engine fired and that the car would have moved except for the crush of spectators. Carl soberly observed that his only goal was to demonstrate the S-D's sturdy construction.

A year later—amid such fanfare that thousands of people stopped what they were doing to crane their heads in wonder—Fisher pulled off another bizarre stunt.

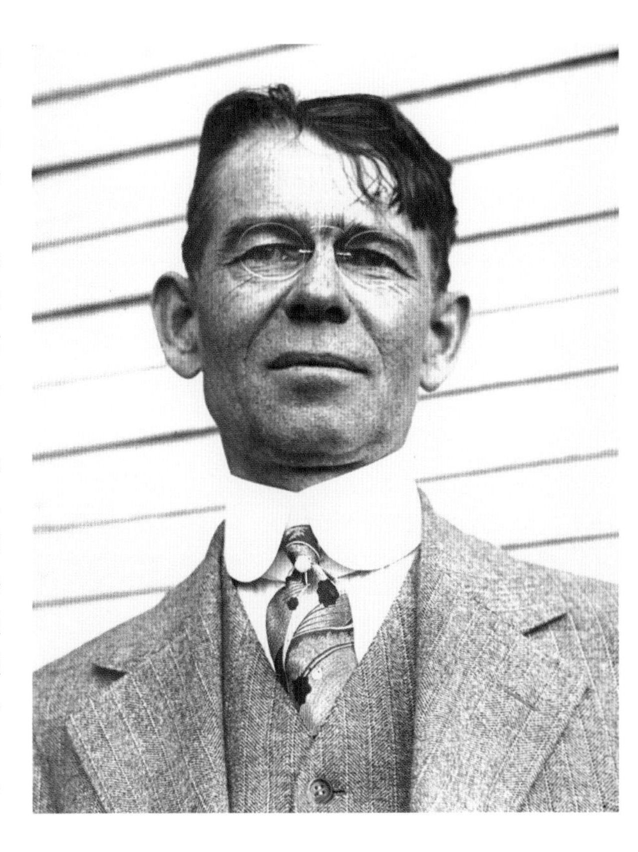

**Arthur C. Newby: One of the four original Speedway partners, his association with Carl Fisher goes back to their bike racing days in the 1890s.**

Imagine a five-acre wooden salad bowl with a quarter-mile track around the bottom and seating for 15,000. That's the super-size bicycle-racing facility Carl Fisher persuades Arthur Newby to build in 1898 three miles north of downtown Indianapolis to host the national convention of the League of American Wheelmen. Just a year later, cars are in and bikes are out, and Newby tears down his wooden palace.

James Allison: A principal partner along with Carl Fisher in the Indianapolis Motor Speedway Co., Allison is the calmer, more thoughtful of the two. The small machine shop he opens near the track in 1915 would grow into the Allison Division of General Motors.

Frank Wheeler: A risk-taker in the same vein as Carl Fisher, Wheeler is another of the original Speedway partners. He is said to have made and lost several fortunes in the early 1900s.

On Nov. 8, 1908, he and a ballooning buddy, G. L. Bumbaugh, floated across Indianapolis and off into the country in a new-model Stoddard-Dayton touring car which had been suspended to the underside of an enormous gas-filled balloon. The pictures made the papers everywhere.

While thousands watch, Carl Fisher introduces a new Stoddard-Dayton automobile by suspending it from a balloon and floating across Indianapolis in the late afternoon, October 30, 1908. The headline in newspaper ads the next day say: "Stoddard-Dayton is the first car to fly over Indianapolis. It should be your first car." *Spencer Riggs collection*

Jane Watts, who may or may not have been 14 at the time (she said so, but there's evidence she was really 24), recounts in her autobiography the mesmerizing sight. She wrote that she had been keeping a scrapbook devoted to Fisher, whom she had never met. Within a year, she would be his wife.

As a final flourish to his flying car caper, Fisher had declared that he would drive the vehicle back to the city with the balloon folded in back. And that's what he did, except it wasn't the same car. To save weight, the so-called "flight car" had been shorn of its engine and many other heavy parts.

A conspirator was at the landing zone with a similar vehicle, and that's the one Carl drove back to town and displayed to an overflow crowd later that day in his dealership. The slight-of-hand went unreported until Fisher, himself, broke the news.

The 1908-09 period saw Fisher firing on all cylinders. He was 34 years old. He was famous. He had money. For the first time in his life he could see pretty well, as eyeglasses had finally resolved his astigmatism. As one of Indy's more eligible bachelors, it appears he had a robust social life. His sudden marriage to Jane, for instance, prompted Gertrude Hassler, a professional singer and Carl's longtime girlfriend, to sue him for breach of promise. She won.

Then, there was Prest-O-Lite—the firm Fisher and ex-bike racing buddy Jim Allison created in 1904 to commercialize a device that made nighttime motoring possible. It was P.C. Avery's idea. He had invented a small refillable canister to store acetylene under great pressure. Mounted on the running board of a car, it fed the gas via high-pressure lines to the headlamps. The brilliant white light produced by opening a valve and striking a match turned night into day. Before that, the pitiful kerosene or carbide gas lights available to motorists were there primarily so the vehicle could be seen. Suddenly, motorists could actually see.

**Looking a lot like an office building of the mid-20th Century, the Prest-O-Lite factory springs up just south of the Speedway in 1913.**

Prest-O-Lite was a gold mine. It made millionaires out of Fisher and Allison, but it was a public relations nightmare. The canisters were safe enough, but refilling them was a delicate feat; make a mistake and the ensuing explosion could knock down buildings.

As the company expanded to the far reaches of the United States, that happened frequently. After a blast in Indianapolis in the summer of 1908, which damaged a nearby infirmary, the city council passed an ordinance prohibiting "charging stations" inside the city limits.

The ban was soon lifted, but in 1911 Fisher and Allison were looking, anyway, for a new Prest-O-Lite factory site well away from the city. It happened to be under their noses. They'd already turned the Pressley property way out west of the city into a monster racetrack. Just across the road to the south was more open land.

In a year, Presto-O-Lite—soon to become a division of Union Carbide—had a new home, and the first lots in what would eventually become the town of Speedway were being platted. A small machine shop Allison would soon build nearby would morph into the Allison Division of General Motors.

The magnetic effect of the Speedway on its surroundings had already begun to take hold.

**Here's the scene in the service department of the Fisher Garage on North Capital in Indianapolis, circa 1905.** *Spencer Riggs collection*

F.P. SMITH & CO.
JOHN R. WELCH
REMOVAL
W.H. ROLLS-SONS

CHAPTER 2

# A $250,000 GAMBLE

Carl Fisher sailed to France in 1905 for the James Gordon Bennett auto race. The French and Italians were building better cars than the Americans and he wanted to know why.

"Dammit," he would say, "Their cars go uphill faster than ours can come down." His own experiences back home with automobiles in constant need of repair left him cursing in frustration.

Carl came back convinced that unless U.S. manufacturers improved their products, the Europeans would take over the market. What domestic carmakers needed, he said time and again, was a big enclosed track where they could test and develop their vehicles before putting them in the hands of the buying public.

**The Hoosier Motor Club, which Carl Fisher helped organize, is having a car show. It's 1908 on Monument Circle in downtown Indianapolis. Notice the horse and buggy moving clockwise at the upper left.** *Bass Photo Co. Collection, Indiana Historical Society*

That's popular race driver Lewis Strang leaning over a dimensionally correct layout of the Speedway in this 1909 photo, at right. One hundred years later, the house in the background is gone, but the barn behind it is still there.

When Fisher returned to Europe in 1907, he visited Brooklands, the brand new 2.75-mile bowl with a banked concrete track near Weybridge in Surrey, England. The Brooklands visit seemed to crystallize Carl's thinking about building a big track in the U.S. On his return, he talked of little else.

His friend, Tom Taggart, a former mayor of Indianapolis and national chairman of the Democratic party, urged him to build a track in the southern Indiana resort area of French Lick, but nobody could find enough level ground.

Meanwhile, Carl groused. And when Carl groused out loud, he used language that would make a longshoreman blush. Jane Watts, the woman Carl would soon marry, said there were two things about him she could never change: 1) his dreadful use of profanity, and 2) his obsession with having spittoons conveniently spotted throughout their various houses.

The Fisher Automobile Co. building near downtown Indianapolis has a scary steep 134-foot wooden ramp attached to an outside wall. It rises at about 30 degrees to the roof. As spectators gawk, Carl Fisher occasionally lines a car up at the bottom and guns it to the top. A typical trip takes about nine seconds, longer if Carl stops along the way to demonstrate the holding power of the brakes.

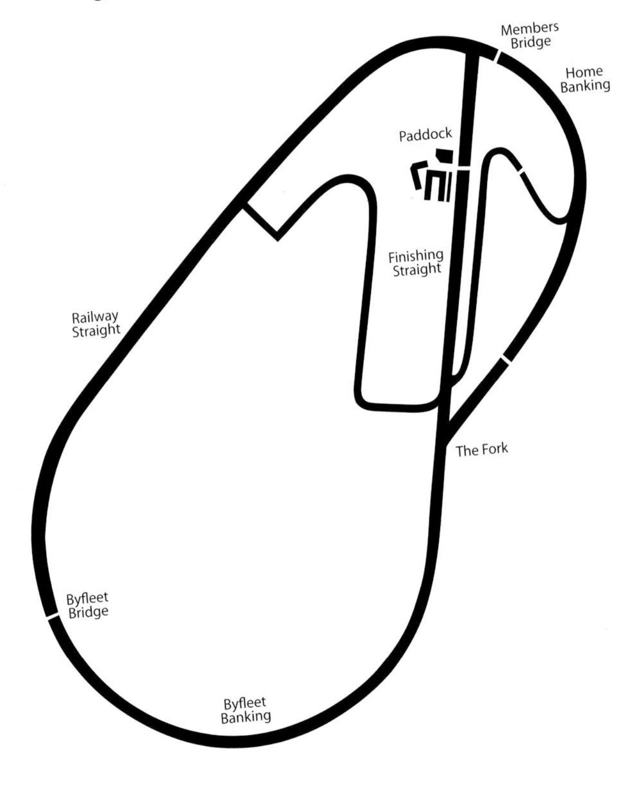


**Brooklands Circuit Layout.**

**The Stoddard-Dayton that may be the very same vehicle Carl Fisher will use to pace three Indy 500s takes a trip around a partly completed track on May 1, 1909.**

# BEAUTIFUL SPEEDWAY CITY

Come Out Saturday and Sunday

In case of death of the purchaser before the lot is fully paid for, this Company will give to his or her heirs or assigns a Warranty Deed if said heirs or assigns will pay one-half the amount of the purchase price still remaining due.

**How to Reach Speedway City**

Take Ben Hur car (all cars stop at Speedway City), get off at the Speedway, walk West one-half square to Main Street, then South on Main Street into the addition.

You will find Salesmen on the ground every day.

Circulars and plats mailed on application.

TERMS

$10 Cash—$10 Per Month

No Interest No Taxes

Quite a number of the people who live here can find employment at their door. Several manufacturing plants are already here and in operation. More to come.

**Beautiful Speedway City**

We invite you to come and see what we are doing. You will be agreeably surprised at the changes taking place. We have commenced at the foundation and are building up. We have prepared the ground so that you can start your home right.

You will find cement walks, curbs, a splendid gravel roadway, forest trees, shade trees, water, gas, electric lights, the streets lighted with gas the same as North Pennsylvania and Meridian Streets, telephone, good interurban service, all cars stop at Speedway City, "Ben Hur line." We are safeguarding the interests of the community by properly regulating the erection of dwellings as to the size and number of rooms in each; also that they shall be built of good material and with a view to architecture and workmanship.

We also keep out all undesirable persons and lines of business. You will find schools, churches and stores.

Come and spend part of the day with us. Bring your lunch, you will find plenty of shade and attractions.

The great Speedway, the greatest automobile oval in the world, is located immediately north of Speedway City.

**Speedway Realty Co.**

614-619 State Life Building

Phones 5348

We ask you to come out and see Speedway City before making a purchase elsewhere. All interurban cars, Ben Hur line, stop at Speedway City.

**Lemon H. Trotter is in his 40s when he negotiates the land deal that produces the Indianapolis Motor Speedway. Trotter then acquires property south and west of the track, and soon this advertisement above appears. The town is billed as one of America's first "horseless" cities, where wide streets are tailor-made for the automobile. Demand for lots is not overwhelming. When the Town of Speedway is incorporated in 1926, there are 67 property owners and 507 people.** *Bass Photo Co. Collection, Indiana Historical Society*

Finally, Lemon H. Trotter, Fisher's real estate agent, had listened long enough. On an autumn day in 1908, the two were enduring a torturous trip from Dayton to Indianapolis. Their car was overheating and blowing tires, and Fisher was in a royal snit. Without adequate test facilities, carmakers were using their customers as guinea pigs, he fussed.

The 40-something Trotter apparently suggested that his client put up or shut up. Maybe a day or two later, Trotter and Fisher motored about five miles out the Crawfordsville Pike (now 16th Street) to where it intersected the Ben Hur inter-urban line and the Big Four Railroad. Trotter pointed to the land the locals called the Pressley farm even though Levi Munter now owned the 80 acres closest to the intersection. The Chenowith family owned 240 acres farther north and east.

"What's the price?" Carl is supposed to have asked. "I'd guess $80,000," said Trotter. "Buy it," said Carl.

Trotter was able to report on Dec. 12 that he had options on both parcels for $72,000. Two months later, March 20, 1909, articles of incorporation were filed for the Indianapolis Motor Speedway Company. It was capitalized at $250,000. Fisher and Allison were in at 30 percent apiece; Newby and Frank H. Wheeler each owned 20 percent.

The partners decided on a two and one half-mile track that was more rectangular than oval. Each turn would be a quarter-mile. The straightaways would be five-eighths of a mile and the two short stretches between the turns would be one-eighth of a mile apiece. Banking would be just nine degrees 12 minutes in each corner.

A great sweeping ribbon that looped gracefully back upon itself in the infield was part of the plan. It would have added another two and one half miles of track and provided spectators at the southwest corner of the main straightaway a close-up view of every car three times in every lap. Although work on the infield course was postponed as the cost of the project began to worry the partners, it was a prominent feature on a widely circulated picture postcard.

**The original track layout.**
*Postcard courtesy of Robin West.*

**VIP spectators are in their Sunday best for opening day in 1909.**

Balloons at far right are readied for the Speedway's first race on June 5, 1909.

Meanwhile, the huge corners and long straights of the big track were taking shape. By late March, the C.C. King Bros. Co. of Montezuma, Indiana, was slicing a 50-foot-wide (60 feet in the turns) rectangular strip around the perimeter of the property. Workmen were also erecting a mammoth covered grandstand with seats for 12,000, and other buildings, including a three-story judge's stand and some special VIP box seats.

Down in the south end, bleachers seating 3,000 were going up for the balloon races Fisher

One of the balloons due to start a race in 1909 is being held down by a few attendants and dozens of sandbags fastened to a netting that completely encloses the bag.

Balloons prepare for lift off in June 1909. It's the first race of any kind at the Speedway.

had in mind, along with an enormous 840,000-cubic-foot (50 x 280 x 60 feet) hanger. Since hydrogen gas would be needed to inflate the balloons, a pipeline was laid from the Indianapolis Gas Company four miles away.

And almost as an afterthought, an 8-foot

**A steam roller at work on the final phase of track construction.** *Library of Congress*

Songwriter Paul Dresser dies in New York in 1906. He wrote "On the Banks of the Wabash Far Away," which was the basis of a 1917 version called simply "Indiana" by James Hanley and Ballard McDonald. Jim Nabors has sung a version of that song, "Back Home Again in Indiana," before almost every Indy 500 since 1972.

tall wooden fence topped with barbed wire was taking shape slat by slat around the outside of the property. Like all the buildings, it would be whitewashed with dark green trim.

Altogether, the place was a beehive of activity. With local newspapers chronicling the progress on a daily basis and hordes of curious onlookers kibitzing, work went on from daylight till dark. About 500 men, plus 300 mules and several steam-powered rollers and graders, rushed to meet an incredibly ambitious deadline.

Not that the job was terribly complicated. Two and a half miles wasn't that far, and the Macadam recipe wasn't much different from what the King brothers were using to improve public roads elsewhere in Indiana.

First, they removed topsoil and established a smooth clay base. Then they applied two inches of creek gravel and rolled it with a 15-ton steam-powered roller. On top of that, they applied two inches of crushed limestone and rolled it with an 8-ton roller. Then, they spread a layer of hot tar and dusted it with one or two inches of crushed stone chips. Finally, they applied another much

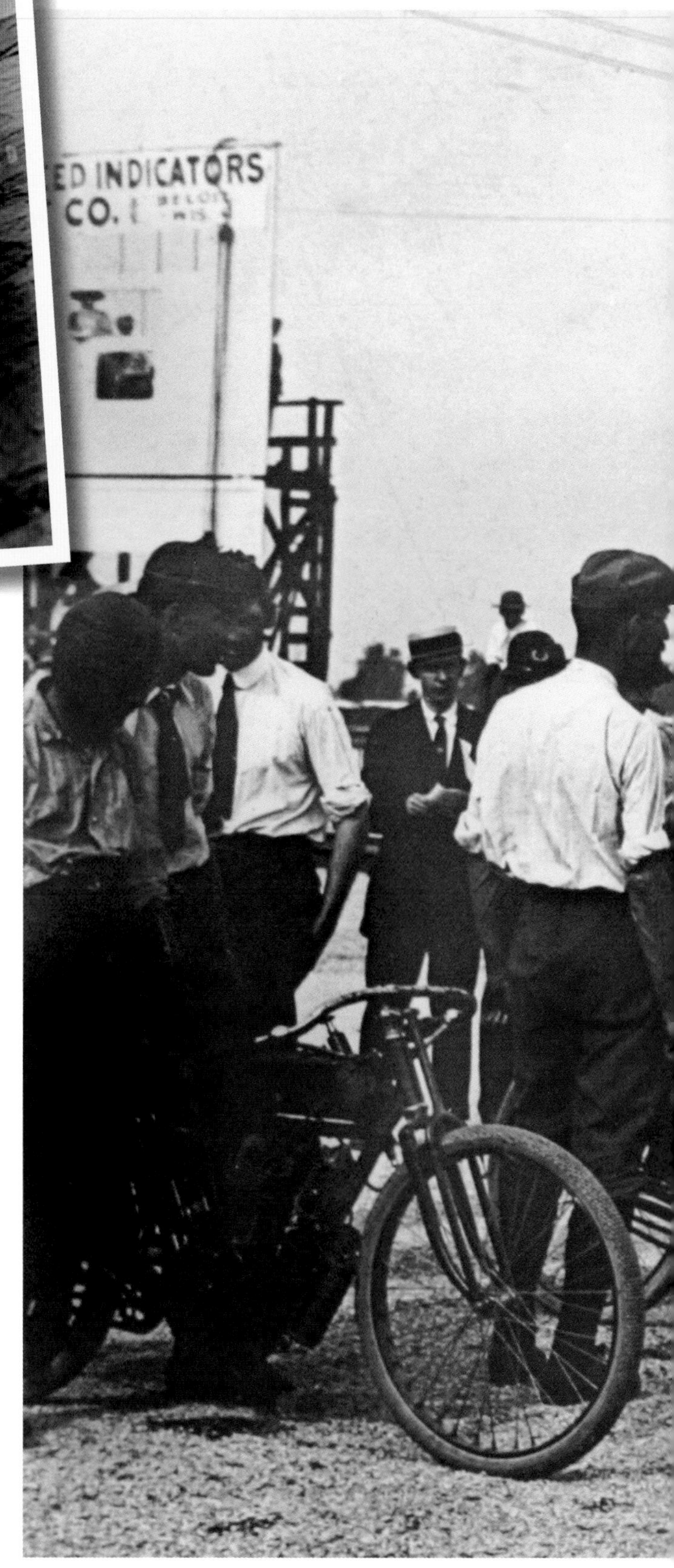

Motorcycle riders line up for the Speedway's first race in 1909.

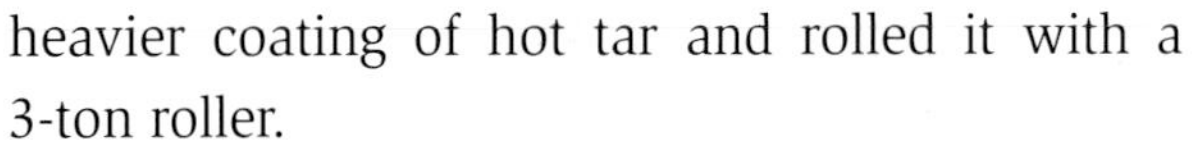

heavier coating of hot tar and rolled it with a 3-ton roller.

Jane said in her book that Carl hovered over the work site like the proud parent of a newborn. It's also possible he spent so much time out there because he was worried about where his money was going. He had happily conspired in many risky ventures, but they paled before this one. And people were already calling it "Fisher's Folly."

Eager to see their investment start paying off, the partners scheduled a national balloon race for June 5, hardly more than six weeks after breaking ground.

Three days of auto races were set for the July 4 weekend, and a round of big national motorcycle races was announced for early August. More auto racing was planned for the Labor Day weekend.

By early May, work was far enough along that Fisher held the first of what would be several thousand press events at the track over the next 100 years.

An iconic photo of Carl wrestling a Stoddard-Dayton loaded with reporters through a rutted turn made newspapers far and wide.

**Carl Fisher at the Harlem racetrack in Chicago, Illinois.**

Carl Fisher's big-league race driving career is over in 1905 before it starts. A brutish machine constructed for him is too heavy for the Vanderbilt Cup race and too powerful for anything but an exhibition race later that year at the Indiana State Fairgrounds.

**Carl Fisher's 1905 Premier race car that's now in the Speedway museum.**

But trouble lurked. Spring rains had been fierce and two bridges taking the track over the small creek in the Southwest corner could not be finished before mid-summer. The balloon races would go on as scheduled, but everything else was questionable. Shortly, the July 4 auto races were backed off to late August.

Fisher was becoming alarmed. In mid-July, he authorized a 24/7 work schedule and had the gas line extended to the inside of the southwest turn. Burners were brought in to provide enough light for work to continue through the night. To illuminate the outside of the turn, Fisher had dozens of Prest-O-Lite canisters delivered. Looking west from downtown Indianapolis, the horizon glowed.

The pace picked up through late July, but some motorcyclists enroute to a race in Cleveland, who stopped by on August 6, were still unhappy with the track condition. They threatened to boycott their upcoming event, but Fisher promised them the track would be ready for practice when they came back on the 12th. To keep the commitment, he needed several railroad tank cars of oil to arrive absolutely no later than the 7th. It was Tuesday morning, the 10th, before the cars showed up.

Over the next 48 hours, Fisher literally willed the track into a sufficient degree of preparedness that Ed Lingenfelder, a prominent cyclist from California, agreed to give it a try.

He rode a brisk 10 laps in 25 minutes without mishap. But Fisher still needed every bit of his considerable powers of persuasion to keep his entire show from being relocated to the Indiana State Fairgrounds.

Racing would start for real the

next day—Friday, the 13th. Three hundred of the fastest motorcyclists in the nation were in town for two days of competition. World records were certain to be broken.

Then, it rained, and it might be the only time in the history of the Speedway that rain was greeted with open arms. Friday's races were postponed to Saturday. Saturday's races were rescheduled for Monday and Fisher's army of men and mules got 24 more hours to work on the track.

But preparation wasn't the issue. What bothered the cyclists was that top layer of crushed rock and the relatively flat turns. Just nine of 13 original entrants lined up for the first race, a 5-miler. Only 10 of 29 entrants ran in the second race, a 1-mile sprint from a starting line in the North end. And so it went.

With the racers reluctant to run and the small crowd growing restless, the schedule of events was altered. A 10-mile match race between two world champion cyclists—the aforementioned Lingelfelder and Jake DeRosier of Massachusetts—was quickly announced. As they roared out of the fourth turn on their second lap, DeRosier's front tire blew. He flew over the handlebars and slid about 30 yards on the oil-soaked shards of rock. The next day the newspapers said spectators "became hysterical."

Racing continued, however. A 10-miler for the Federation of American Motorcyclists national amateur championship was won by a young Indianapolis resident named E.G. Baker. Soon, the world would come to know him as the colorful cross-country speed record holder, "Cannonball" Baker.

But the final event was called off due to lack of entries. Also cancelled were all of Monday's events. Not many in the motorcycle fraternity seemed sorry to see the show shut down.

**Erwin G. "Cannonball" Baker, shown here stirring a little dirt during a record-setting 11-day transcontinental motorcycle ride in 1914, won an amateur event during the 1909 bike races at the Speedway. A native of southeastern Indiana, he drove a Frontenac in the 1922 Indy 500. His solo 53.5-hour cross-country dash in a Graham-Paige in 1933, quickly dubbed the "Cannonball Run," set a record that stood for 40 years and inspired several books, movies and a TV series.**

**Motorcycles are the first motorized racers at Indy in August 1909. It will be 99 years before they are back.**

This is not an optical illusion. Until a major rehab after the 1935 race, the outer few feet of the track carries a more extreme angle in the turns. The concrete wall is perpendicular to the ground, not the track. The design puts racers who get too high in the corner at risk of being launched over the wall.

That's Johnny Aitken in the lead at the start of a race in 1909. Smoke and dust obscure the rear rows.

# CHAPTER 3

# MORE AGONY THAN ECSTASY

In the pause before the storm, here's an eight-abreast start of a free-for-all race in August 1909.

With the cycles gone, Fisher and his partners had just two days to ready the track for its first exposure to auto racing. A three-day card totaling 18 events was set for August 19 through August 21.

The entry list was heartwarming: 65 cars representing 15 different manufacturers. Fisher's dream of a place where carmakers would come to wring out their products was being realized.

This is the hand-written bid on lined notebook paper that got CC King Bros. and Son the contract to build the track on March 11, 1909.

C. C. King, Bros. & Son.

GENERAL CONTRACTORS

Indianapolis Ind March 11th 09

Indianapolis Motor and speedway co

gentelmen

we the undersigned contractors

Propose to grade to subgrade and complete intire

speedway satisfactory to superentendent and oners

of Indianapolis speedway of Indianapolis Indiana.

specifications and Plans "sheets no 5-6-7" for the tolle

sum of Fourteen Thousand seven Hundread & Fifty Dollars

$14.750.00

Borrow meterial to be Obtained within ~~five~~ 6 Hundread

feet limit Hall. or we Propose to grade and complete

same as above mentioned actual yardage from

crossection at Fifteen cents (.15¢)

per cubic yard. Meterial to be Obtained within ~~five~~ Six

Hundread feet limit after which one ~~half~~ cent 1

per cubic yard for each addtional Hundread foot over Hall

work is to be completed within sixty days from signing

of contract Indecent weather to be consitered payments

of work to be made Every Thirty days on or about the

first of Each month to the Extent of Eighty per cent of

yardage Moved ballance of Estimates to be paid when

C. C. King, Bros. & Son.

GENERAL CONTRACTORS

work is completed and excepted by the superentend

and Owners of same

CC King Bros & son

address Sherman House

Indianapolis Indiana

That the automobile has practically reached the limit of its development is suggested by the fact that during the past year no improvements of a radical nature have been introduced. — *Scientific American, 1909*

Barney Oldfield set quick time in practice with a lap of 76.27 miles an hour and other drivers were soon running over 70 mph. But as the day went on, the dusty track began falling apart. At 3 p.m., Fisher stopped practice in order for workmen to patch the ruts and lay down more oil. They worked all night.

When the gates opened at 9 a.m. the next day, spectators saw horse-drawn tank wagons still oiling the track in front of the grandstand, but they also saw a carnival scene so vast and colorful it boggled the mind. There were flags and pennants flying by the hundreds from the roofs of every building. A long row of tents housed dozens of auto-related displays, including a gold-plated Overland automobile, which was to be awarded at the end of the 1909 season to the driver with the fastest time in a measured mile.

There was marked parking for 10,000 cars and 3,000 horse-drawn carriages. Tickets cost 50 cents to $1.50. A special train brought people from the Stoddard-Dayton plant in Ohio. Huge car caravans originating in Chicago, St. Louis, Cincinnati and other Midwestern cities descended upon the intersection of Crawfordsville Pike and Georgetown Road.

The grandstands were packed by noon. Although most people brought their lunches, concessions stands did a land-office business. Soda pop was selling for the rip-off sum of 10 cents a bottle until Ernest Moross, the director of events, ordered the price capped at 5 cents.

The start of the first event was delayed while state militiamen prodded several hundred people off a pedestrian bridge spanning the track 200 yards north of the grandstand.

The bridge was where the cars lined up before accelerating across the starting line in what was supposed to be a flying start. But the disciplined run-up to the line degenerated into a mad dash, so Fred "Pop" Wagner, the flagman, brought everybody back for a standing start.

Louis Schwitzer quickly grabbed the lead in his Stoddard-Dayton. He stayed there for both laps and took the black and white checkered flag to the wild delight of the trainload of S-D people from Dayton, who were jammed into the grandstand nearby.

Schwitzer made history. He was the first winner of the first automobile race at the Speedway, but if the men with the megaphones who were calling the races made anything special out of it, the next day's papers missed it.

The second race of the day saw another ragged run-up to the line, so Wagner again ordered a standing start. This time it was Louis Chevrolet ahead at the end.

Carl Fisher's former bike racing buddy was already a motor racing superstar. He was a member of the Buick racing team—the most formidable of all U.S. factory racing operations—and would soon partner with a one-time buggy maker named William C. "Billy" Durant, in a car-building venture bearing his name.

The Chevrolet Motor Co. was formed in 1911. It was producing a million cars a year by 1916, but Louis was long gone. The pair disagreed often over everything from car design to smoking habits. They split in 1914, and Louis abandoned his name and his financial stake to Durant in 1914.

Of course, the company prospered. Durant, who had founded General Motors in 1908 and lost it to his creditors two years later, leveraged Chevrolet stock to regain control of GM in 1916. One of his first acts was to make Chevrolet a division of GM.

Louis got nothing out of the deal. But by then, he and his

**When Carl Fisher searches in 1909 for the most renowned flagman in motor racing, he looks no farther than Fred "Pop" Wagner. The flamboyant Easterner is as iron-willed as he is colorful. He and Carl are in frequent disagreement, but Wagner stays aboard for four years.**

**The public address system in 1910 is this huge megaphone. It isn't known how the announcer was selected, or if anybody heard him over the din.**

held at the starting line for 85 seconds after Ray Harroun's little Marmon was flagged off. He was leading the feature event—the 250-mile Prest-O-Lite trophy race—when a flying rock broke his goggles, sending a shower of tar, dust and slivers of glass into his eyes.

Not long after Chevrolet was led bleeding from his Buick, tragedy struck Wilfred Bourque and his riding mechanic, Harry Holcomb. Something seemed to break on their powerful Knox and the car careened into a ditch before turning over against a fence. They were the new Speedway's first fatalities. An emergency crew removed the wreckage while racecars thundered by.

Four hours and 39 minutes after the start, it was the Buick team's Bob Burman ahead at the end.

By now the track was in such bad shape, officials of the American Automobile Association considered canceling the next two days' events. But Carl's persuasive skills won out again, and his army of workmen began another all-night repair session.

Day 2 saw an estimated 20,000 people on hand to witness Barney Oldfield's Speedway racing debut. It was painful. While still on his first lap, a carburetor fire burned the leather straps retaining the hood on Oldfield's mighty National. His arm was badly cut when he raised it to protect his head as the hood blew past.

Oldfield was back for Race 6, but hurting. He lost control of his Benz and it slid off the track.

The crowd for a hot and humid day 3 was huge; the papers estimated 35,000. It was standing room only under the grandstand roof.

People stood eight deep along the fence for a half-mile to the north. Most were in their Sunday best—men in shirts and ties and straw hats, women in long dresses carrying parasols. Armed militiamen patrolled the environs.

**This 1909 photo of a smiling Louis Chevrolet catches him out of uniform. He's bundled up to ward off flying stones, but in full racing regalia, he would also be wearing goggles and heavy gloves.**

brothers, Art and Gaston, had established themselves in the nascent racing industry, which had sprung up around the Brickyard.

They gained fame, if not fortune, driving, designing and building cars and engines for many years.

Not that Louis could be much busier than he was on opening day at the track in 1909. He won Race 2. He was closing in on fellow Buick team driver Bob Burman for second when the checker was thrown in Race 3. He ran fourth in Race 4, a 4-lap handicap event that saw his big Buick

His arm still bandaged, Oldfield gave the crowd its money's worth in Race 3—a 25-mile contest for one of the most coveted prizes in motor sport—the Remy Grand Brassard (French for arm shield.) It was Frank Remy's idea. The millionaire magneto manufacturer from nearby Anderson, Indiana, bankrolled the race. The winner this year got to keep the shield along with a $75-a-week stipend as long as he continued to win future Grand Brassard races. There was silver in the arm shield, but to many a poor driver, the money was what counted.

The race was a cakewalk for Oldfield, who set world records at every five-mile increment.

The big event of the day, however, was the 300-mile race for the $10,000 Wheeler-Schebler Trophy. Frank Wheeler, one of the four Speedway partners, designed it. The 7-1/2-foot silver cup is now housed at the Speedway's Hall of Fame Museum.

The track was already deteriorating as 19 cars started the race at 1:30 p.m. By 6 p.m., a riding

**Bob Burman.** *Library of Congress*

Marie Chomel (AKA Betty Blythe, a reporter for *The Indianapolis Star*) is believed the first woman to complete a lap of the Speedway at near racing speed in 1909. "I was trussed up in heavy clothing topped off by a hood made of leather with an Isinglass window, and helped into a stripped-down stock car with just a board for a seat," she wrote. "Bob Burman drove me. Two drivers were killed that day, and I thought I would die before I completed the two laps at a terrific speed with gravel hitting the Isinglass like hailstones." Her story is credited with a last-minute surge in ticket sales for the next day's racing.

**When a tire blows during practice on May 30, 1910, Ray Harroun rides this car 110 feet astraddle a concrete wall and through a fence. He's back later that day to win two races. Then, he announces his retirement. It is not permanent. Exactly one year later, he wins the first Indianapolis 500.**

**Ray Harroun races by the Pagoda in a 1910 event, shortly before he announces his retirement. He comes back in 1911 to win the first Indy 500 in a car that looks almost identical to this one, but his 1911 vehicle has a rear view mirror and longer tail.**

mechanic and two spectators would be dead, several people would be injured, and the race would be halted at 235 miles.

Jane Watts Fisher (she and Carl were married on October 23, 1908) witnessed the scene from her box seat.

"Every minute held dramas of tragedy, mutilation and death. Cars skidded off the buckling macadam and burst into flame," she wrote. "I watched Carl's face grow whiter. As the death toll mounted, he stopped the race."

Other accounts indicate it was Wagner who halted the action over Carl's strenuous objections.

**The 1st National Aviation Meet, Indianapolis Motor Speedway, June 13-18, 1910. This is actually a "doctored" photograph. There were only a couple of occasions on which there were even two aircraft in the air at the same time. Virtually all of the runs were solo.** *Library of Congress*

Indianapolis, Ind., July 6, 1909.

The Indianapolis Speedway,

Indianapolis, Ind.

Gentlemen:-

We hereby agree to furnish material and service for building five miles roadway according to specifications and terms hereinafter mentioned.

Furnish Taroid H, a road binder made of pure coal tar that will produce a road similar to specimen road built in garage July 5th, 1909. This material hrdens quickly and remains solid.

Furnish one tank suitable for heating Taroid, also furnish two tank wagons for hauling Taroid from heating tank to roadway.

Furnish Mr. Hall for two or three days when work is ready to start to instruct the workmen in the preparation of roadway an application of Taroid, and once per week thereafter during construction.

Furnish one-half dozen puuring cans suitable for applying Taroid. The freight on the heating tank and tank wagons to and from Indianapolis to be paid by Indianapolis Speedway.

Furnish two men, one for handling heating tank, one for applying Taroid on road. These men to be paid by the Indianapolis Speedway at the rate of Twenty-fice Cents per hour. Railroad fare also to be paid.

Taroid to be shipped in barrels and gallonage to be compudted on gross weight of package at ten pounds per gallon.

All other expense such as unloading cars, hauling and applying Taroid, preparation of roadway, setting equipment to be paid for by Indianapolis Speedway. We agree to keep sufficient Taroid on hand to properly prosecute work except under conditions over which we have no control.

Price to be Five Cents (5) per gallon F.O.B. cars Indianapolis.

Terms 2% discount for cash in ten days or net cash thirty days after shipment.

F. J. LEWIS MFG. COMPANY.

W H Lewis Vice President

**From the Speedway archives, here's the July 6, 1909 contract for constructing the first track surface.**

Huge construction cost overruns in 1909 have the Speedway partnership reeling from the get-go. The project is budgeted at $250,000. It ends up costing about $350,000. A half million yards of dirt must be moved. The track surface requires 300,000 gallons of tar. Four hundred workmen live in camps on the site.

Medics are at the ready in 1910. Notice the canister attached to the underside of the ambulance; it contains acetylene, which fuels those massive headlamps. Carl Fisher's Prest-O-Lite company has a corner on the canister market nationwide.

CHAPTER 4

# TO BRICK, OR NOT TO BRICK

**Beer ads and weird paint schemes on racecars existed in 1911, too.**

The misfortunes attending Indy's inaugural auto races produced some serious second guessing about the future of racing at the Speedway.

A wave of criticism from newspapers followed the accidents. *The Detroit News* weighed in with the hope that track racing on big circuits like the Speedway would not recover from the black eye it received at Indianapolis.

One of the most significant documents in Speedway history spells out terms and prices for the bricks to be laid in the fall of 1909.

Veedersburg, Ind. September 14th, 1909.

Indianapolis Motor Speedway Co.,
Indianapolis, Ind.

Gentlemen:

We propose to furnish you sufficient of our Culver Blocks to pave your Speedway course, adjacent to the Big 4 Tracks, west of the city of Indianapolis. According to the estimate of your engineer, Mr. Andrews, about three million, one hundred thousand (3,100,000) blocks will be required for the work.

The price of the blocks is to be Thirteen Dollars ($13.00)per thousand, f.o.b., cars, your switch, Big 4 tracks.

Terms: Net, 10 days from date of invoice, invoice to be rendered at the end of every week for the consignments of that week.

Should you decide to use what Alley Blocks we have in stock, the price will be Eleven Dollars ($11.00) per thousand, f.o.b., your switch; terms, same as above.

Under this proposal, we will furnish you from two million to 2,500,000 of the larger size Culver Blocks (one car load of which was shipped you and is being tested on your course), which were shown your Mr. Fisher when he visited our yard on September 12th: the balance will be supplied from our regular size Culver Blocks (slightly narrower), unless you elect to take what Alley Blocks we have - 2 cars of which were shipped you and are being tested on your track.

You are to pay all freights on the blocks and return expense bills promptly to the Wabash Clay Company for credit on your account.

All blocks furnished under this proposal are guaranteed by us to be free from lime in sufficient quantities to cause disintegration, and from cracks or flaws which will cause disintegration from freezing and thawing. See addendum

It is understood that, should you order more blocks than are required to complete your work, the surplus blocks will be your property and you are to pay for them as though used on your Speedway.

It is understood that we are to begin shipments upon your order and continue same at the rate of not exceeding 20 cars per day until the

John Jenkins in the Schacht Motor Car Co. number 18 in 1913.

The Indianapolis Motor Speedway and the America of the early 1900s are made for each other. Historians will label the first 10 years of the 20th Century the "Progressive Age." In today's vernacular, it might best be called the "Macho Age." It is all about technical innovation, personal ambition, the virtues of masculinity and the will to win. As an expression of those values, the Speedway of 1909 has three things going for it: 1) It's a laboratory to test the latest, greatest example of consumer technology – the automobile, 2) It's an arena where men could test their courage and skill against themselves and each other, and 3) It's a theater where thrill-seeking spectators get to watch daredevil racers risk life and limb.

It really didn't matter whether the partners agreed with the critics; they were in no position to bail out. Their personal fortunes were on the line and they had to make the monstrous facility pay off. It appears they were also eager to dispel a notion that the Speedway project suffered from shoddy design and workmanship.

If there was any good to come from the calamities of August, it might have been the genuine commitment the Fisher group would display from then on to the safety and security of competitors and spectators alike.

contract is filled. However, it is agreed that we shall not be responsible for delays caused by shortage of cars or other things beyond our power to control.

Upon the following conditions we will allow you a special discount of Fifty Cents (.50c) per thousand on all blocks furnished under this proposal: In all your advertisements, write ups, (where practicable) race announcements and other literature issued prior to January 1st, 1911 on account of The Indianapolis Motor Speedway, you are to state that the Speedway is paved with Culver Blocks, and, when practicable, you are also to state that they were selected by your Management, only after thorough tests had been made of several other materials, and other forms of pavement rigidly inspected. The matter of deciding when and where such statements are practicable we will cheerfully leave entirely in your hands. You are also to grant us permission to erect and maintain on your grounds, at a suitable place, a "board", not to exceed 20' x 50', advertising the fact that the Speedway is paved with Culver Blocks,-the location of the "board" and the advertisement on it to be approved by your president.

One of the chief inducements in making you the unusally low quotations we have is the advertisement our Culver Blocks will receive from being used exclusively in paving your Speedway. The success of the pavement depends largely upon care in its construction: therefore, this proposal is based upon the assumption that at least the same degree of care will be shown in rolling and filling the blocks upon the entire Speedway as was exercised in the experimental section put down last week, under the supervision of Mr. Andrews.

The Wabash Clay Company,

By R. D. Culver Pres't.

Accepted: Indianapolis, Ind.

September 16 1909.

Indianapolis Motor Speedway Co

By Carl G. Fisher Pres IMS Co

James A. Allison Secy & Treas.

ADDENDUM.

In unloading the Blocks from the cars, it is understood that your men will use brick clamps and not pitch the Blocks into the wagons; also that the Blocks will be carefully unloaded by hand from the wagons and neatly piled at points convenient for use, but where they will not come in contact with clay or mud, in sufficient quanities to endanger the adhesion of the cement filler, when it is applied to the pavement.

Our guarantee, on the first page of this proposal, is for a period of five years from the completion of the pavement and is simply conditioned on your rolling and tamping the Blocks, applying the cement grout filler, and protecting it after it is applied, according to the No.1 Specifications of the National Paving Brick Manufacturers' Association, part of which are hereto attached, as far as same are applicable to your track. On those conditions, we will replace, without cost to you, any Blocks that prove defective under our guarantee.

The present bituminous-rock foundation, properly rolled, is acceptable to us.

Any misunderstanding or disagreement arising under this proposal shall be settled by arbitration in the following manner, each party hereto shall select one arbitrator, these two arbitrators shall select a third, and a decision of a majority of the arbitrators so chosen shall be final and binding on both parties hereto.

Mark Foster says in his 2000 Fisher biography, *Castles in the Sand,* that Carl was determined not only to make the Speedway as safe as humanly possible but to make it the finest in the world, a state-of-the-art facility that would attract the greatest international racers.

First of all, the track had to be paved. That was a given. The material of choice would be bricks—3.2 million of them.

Within 30 days, the partners had conducted some primitive tests. One involved roping Johnny Aitken's racecar to a small section of brick and engaging the clutch. (The wheels spun and the tires smoked, but the bricks stayed put.) Soon, the Wabash Clay Company in western Indiana had a contract to deliver the necessary quantity. To fill the order on time, Wabash subcontracted with several other local brick manufacturers.

A yellowed three-page purchase agreement now tucked away at the Speedway's Hall of Fame Museum stipulated the price: 13 cents apiece. The first bricks were off-loaded from two rail cars September 18.

Choreographing the trip from the kiln to the

Paving bricks are stacked outside Turn 1. Notice the foundation for the concrete wall.

It appears precise instructions for mixing and applying the slurry are being followed to the letter.

The paving process moves along the main straightaway. Notice the brick carriers.

track was a feat by itself. The bricks came to the Ben Hur station on the Speedway's southwest corner. They were carefully stacked on horse-drawn carts and hauled to where they were needed around the track. A moveable conveyer assembly was then employed to deposit bricks within arm's reach of workmen.

Just 63 days after paving began, the job was done. In addition, Fisher had ordered a concrete wall built around part of the track and a 1.5-mile "aeroplane" landing strip graded down the middle of the infield. Anticipating nighttime use of the track, he also purchased enough gas lights to place them 20 feet apart completely around the course.

Braving high winds and bitter cold, 500 spectators showed up a few days before Christmas to watch Indiana Governor Thomas Marshall lay the last brick and several prominent drivers test the new surface.

Despite the weather, it appears a pretty good time was had by all. Walter Christie set a new American record for the quarter-mile of 8.37

**Thomas Marshall.** *Library of Congress*

**The Wright Brothers, Wilbur and Orville, are the big draw for Carl Fisher's air show at the Speedway in 1910.**

seconds. Lewis Strang broke Barney Oldfield's one-mile Speedway record with a time of 40.61 seconds, then came back the next day to clock a 39.21.

By spring 1910, another grandstand had gone up and three 25-foot-long scoreboards erected. There were catwalks behind the boards to accommodate the people responsible for changing numbers and a "foreman" with a telephone headset wired to the judges' stand.

Perhaps unable to control his P.T. Barnum instincts, Fisher opened the season in late March with what can best be described as a battery of county fair stunts. Local carmakers were persuaded to come on out and showcase their cars in such antics as a potato race, where 10 baskets were set up along the track. A passenger in each car was supposed to toss a potato into each basket as the driver sped by. The papers said 5,000 people watched.

The 1910 Speedway racing calendar was already set. There would be auto races in May, July, August and September, an aviation meet in June and a balloon race in August.

The new bricks got their first real test over the Memorial Day weekend, when 24 races were held over three days. Barney Oldfield was back, along with Chevrolet, Strang, Johnny Aitken, and a large contingent of race drivers eager to test themselves at what was already being called the "Brickyard."

**Some flying action from the Wilbur and Orville Wright show.**

Among them was a diminutive engineer with the Nordyke & Marmon Car Company named Ray Harroun, who would win the Wheeler-Schebler Trophy race on Day 2 and the 50-lap Remy Grand Brassard race on Day 3, hours after surviving a horrendous crash in another car. But his greatest Speedway win was exactly one year away.

An estimated 60,000 spectators packed the grandstands and crowded around the fences on the final day of the meet. The partners were pleased.

Next up was the aviation meet. Air shows were rare events in the early 1900s, and this one featured the Wright Brothers themselves, so Speedway management expected a big turnout. But only 2,000 paying customers appeared for Day 1, which included an early evening flight with Orville Wright at the controls and Carl Fisher his passenger.

Maybe 19,000 were on hand the next day. Attendance declined every day through the remainder of the weeklong event, even though some of America's most celebrated pilots were taking part in various exhibitions and races.

Another product of Carl Fisher's P.T. Barnum imagination, his "wind wagon" is a propeller-driven vehicle built to race an airplane during the aviation meet of 1910.

A precursor to its famous blimp, Goodyear brings this balloon to the Speedway in 1910.

Eager to upstage and out-flank other super speedways then on the drawing boards, the Carl Fisher partnership makes history on September 7, 1910, with an announcement that a 500-mile race next May will pit American cars against the best of Europe. Prize money will amount to an astounding $25,000.

Fisher thought the low turnout wasn't for lack of interest but rather a matter of common sense: Why buy a ticket when you could stay outside for free and see almost as much of the show?

When July's round of 24 auto races over three days rolled around, the grandstands had been enlarged again; this time to hold 50,000, but just 5,000 were on hand on Day 1 and less on Day 2.

Day 3 was Independence Day. A heat wave with temperatures in the high 90s had been broken by an early morning shower. The driver lineup read like a who's-who of American auto racing. It was turning into a perfect summer day, and the track braced for a record crowd; however, only 20,000 showed up.

Soon afterward, a disappointed Fisher announced both August events would be cancelled and the September auto racing show shortened by one day. The year was not turning out as expected. Where were last year's enormous Speedway crowds?

No question cars were more than ever on the public mind; fast cars, especially. Barney Oldfield's world speed record of 131.724 mph at Daytona in the spring was big news in Indianapolis.

In Detroit, Henry Ford's low-priced Model T was now in full production, and the working class could dare to dream of owning one. In Indiana and throughout America, the love affair with all things automobile was heating up.

But there was worry at the Brickyard.

The Labor Day weekend had 20 race events scheduled over two days. Except for the haze from giant wildfires burning in Idaho and Montana, the weather was nice.

The Buick team was missing, but in all, 25 drivers representing 20 different car manufacturers were signed up, but just a few thousand spectators were in the stands when Saturday's Day 1 racing began.

Sunday was a day off. Monday was Labor Day. When "Pop" Wagner started the first of the Day 2 races about 1:20 p.m., an estimated 70,000 people were five miles away watching the Labor Day parade in downtown Indianapolis.

**Race driver Bill Endicott at the reins.**

The crowd at the track was around 15,000.

There would be more racing at the Speedway in 1910—balloons this time.

There was also the National Aviation Meet, which the Wright Brothers attended. But Carl Fisher was thinking about next year. He needed a gimmick bigger than anything he had dreamed up in his wildest "Crazy Carl" days.

In his book, *500 Miles to Go,* Al Bloemker relates the following Fisher/Allison conversation:

Fisher: "If we expect to draw big crowds, we're going to have to give the people something different—something they can't see any place except Indianapolis."

Allison: "We're giving the public too much racing. If we cut down on the number and increase the price of tickets, we'll be better of in the long run."

Fisher: "See what the boys think about one big race a year."

Cars race under a backstretch bridge in the early days.

Burning low-quality low-octane gasoline causes the curtain of smoke as cars line up seven-wide for the start in a 1910 race.

# It's Party Time

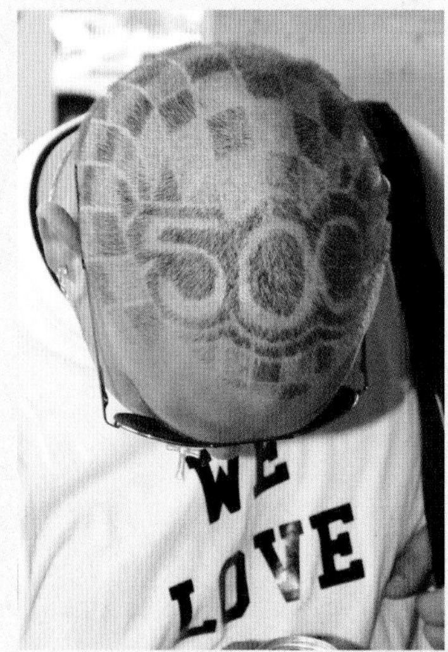

**If you really try, it's not hard to stand out in a crowd, whether having a "500" shaved on your head or wearing a very tall checkerboard hat.**

From the time Carl Fisher opened its gates in 1909, the Speedway had been a party place. But in the beginning, decorum ruled. The Sunday clothes everybody seemed to be wearing must have been a factor, and it helped that armed militiamen were on guard inside the track.

Outside, keeping order was a local law enforcement responsibility. That wasn't difficult at first since the big crowds were five miles away in downtown Indianapolis.

As the area around the track developed, revelers made the corner of 16th and Georgetown Road the epicenter of the party.

While Prohibition was in effect from 1920 to 1933, pre-race newspaper coverage routinely included a warning that federal agents would be prowling the environs on the lookout for miscreants. With repeal, the night-before-the-500 party atmosphere really blossomed.

The carnivals were back after WW II, but as a welcome distraction along with them came the West Sixteenth Street Midget Speedway. It gave fun seekers something else to do.

The little quarter-mile paved oval was a busy place from spring through fall. The Speedway High School football team even played some games there. But the biggest event by far was the triple-header the night before the 500.

There were three complete midget racing programs lasting maybe three hours apiece. Each required a separate admission. So you left after one program was over and bought a new ticket for the next one.

By the mid-'50s, the chain-link fence around the little track was sufficiently saggy that sneaking under it became de rigueur.

The last feature race usually ended a couple of hours before the gates opened at the big track across the street.

They closed the little place in 1958 and replaced it with a shopping center. About that time the town of Speedway had stopped issuing many permits, so some of the carny atmosphere was gone. But the revelry continued.

Marion County's jail bus was a constant presence.

The next 30 years saw the all-night street party ebb and flow.

As the race became more family oriented in the '90s, pre-race partying became more subdued.

The 2008 situation seemed to continue the trend. A 2 a.m. view from the epicenter was nowhere near as unappealing as it was 30 years earlier.

According to Bloemker, Fisher got the partners together a couple of weeks later. They agreed on one race of 500 miles. They agreed entry fees should go up, from as little as $5 in 1910 to $500 in 1911. They also agreed the prize fund had to be enormous. "Hell," said Fisher, "we're talking about the greatest automobile race ever put on anywhere on the face of the earth. Everything connected with it is going to have to be bigger and better than ever before..."

And they agreed on the date of the inaugural 500: May 30, 1911.

**The Wheeler-Schebler Trophy is on display in 1910 as Ray Harroun stops at the line.**

They've made it through the main gate and now these cars thread their way north between the grandstand and the Georgetown Pike fence. It's 1911, and they're probably headed to the crossover and a nice parking spot in the infield before the start of the very first Indy 500.

CHAPTER 5

# FLOUNDERING NO MORE

**From infancy, the flying wing-and-wheel has been a signature logo of the Indianapolis Motor Speedway. Covers of the first two Indy 500 programs in 1911 and '12 are identical.**

The *buzz* around the 500-mile race Carl Fisher slated for his Indianapolis Motor Speedway on Decoration Day, 1911, had been building for six months. His publicity agents were spreading the word throughout North America and Europe.

Attracted by the announced purse of $25,000 (it eventually reached a princely $27,500), entry applications began arriving six months before the race. It helped that starting position would be determined by the date of the entry. The J.I. Case Threshing Machine Co. entry for Lewis Strang was first, so he started on the pole.

Construction projects at the track, including two more huge grandstands, were often in the news. A steady stream of ticket buyers stopped by the little office on North Capital Avenue where T.E. "Pop" Myers and his secretary Eloise "Dolly" Dallenbach held forth.

Fisher had been telling anybody who would listen that the crowd would be stupendous, but the avalanche of humanity descending upon the city in the days and hours before the Tuesday, May 30, race was still quite a sight. There was very little in the immediate vicinity of the track except farmland, so early arrivals zeroed in on downtown Indianapolis five miles to the southeast.

"Never before in its history has the city entertained a larger throng. Never has there been a more cosmopolitan crowd…," gushed *The Indianapolis News.*

Most of the estimated 80,000 people on hand for the 1911 race watch from the comfort of one of those enormous grandstands along the main straightaway.

# INDIANAPOLIS MOTOR SPEEDWAY RESERVATION CHART

**International Sweepstakes 500-Mile Race, Decoration Day, May 30, 1911**

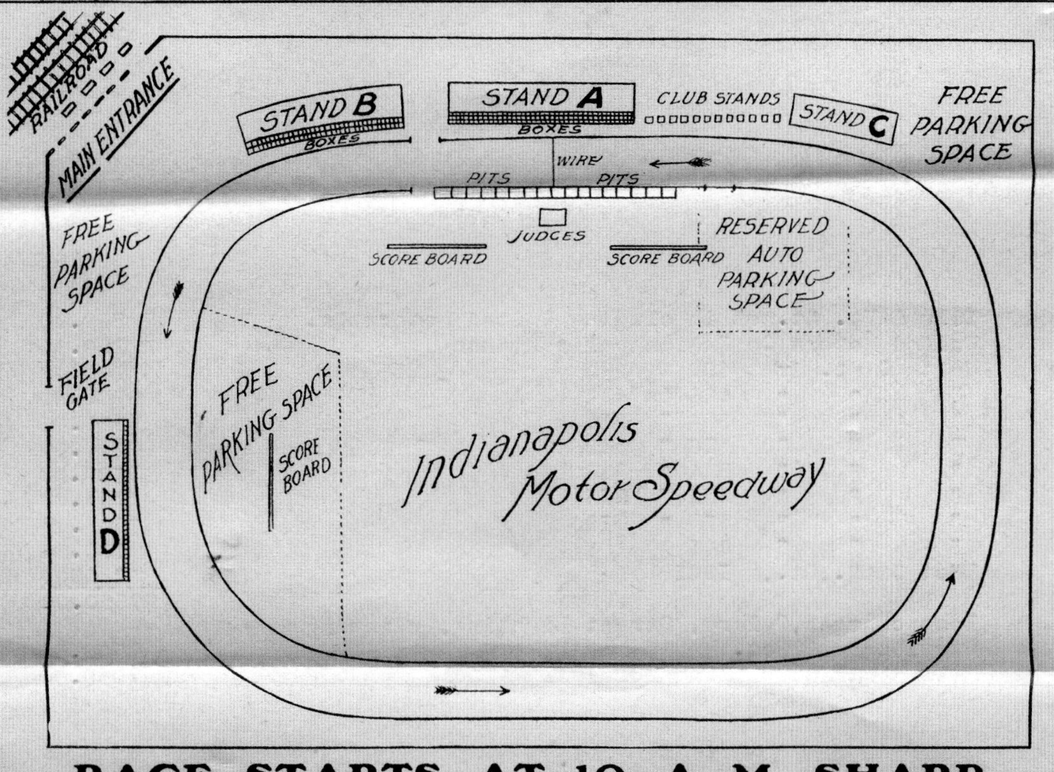


## RACE STARTS AT 10 A. M. SHARP

**General Admission at Main Entrance . $1.00** **General Admission at Field Gate . 50 cents**

MAIN ENTRANCE STANDS A—B—C FIELD GATE STAND D

**Seat Prices are in Addition to General Admission Charges**

| | |
|---|---|
| **Boxes**—Six Seats to Each Box—(In addition to $1.00 admission for each person) | **$24.00** |
| **Single Box Seats**—(In addition to $1.00 admission) | **4.00** |
| **Club Stands**—Seating 20 Persons—(In addition to $1.00 admission for each person) | **50.00** |
| **Seats In Stand A**—(In addition to $1.00 admission) | **1.50** |
| **Seats In Stand B**—(In addition to $1.00 admission) | **1.00** |
| **Seats In Stand D**—(In addition to 50 cents admission) Seats in Stand D are not reserved. | **.50** |
| **Seats In Stand C**—(In addition to $1.00 admission) Seats in Stand C are not reserved. | **Free** |
| **Parking Space**—Charge is in addition to general admission. Reserved Parking Space, per automobile All other parking space is free. | **$2.00** |

**Remittance Must Accompany All Reservations**

Reservations will be filled in the order received.

The Speedway management reserves the right to reject any reservation and refund all money paid on same.

If the seats specified in any reservation order have been sold before receipt of that order, the Speedway management assumes the right to assign other seats as near as possible to those desired, unless return of remittance is requested in such event at time order is placed.

Patrons should specify first, second and third choice in seats when making reservations.

Tickets will be forwarded to purchaser as soon as reservation has been made. It is important that a correct address be furnished by each purchaser as no responsibility for loss of tickets in mail will be assumed by the Speedway management.

**Make all checks, drafts and money orders payable to J. A. Allison, Secretary, Indianapolis Motor Speedway, Indianapolis, Ind.**

**If you are moved by this "flyer" to buy a ticket to the very first Indianapolis 500, you are instructed to make your check payable to J. A. Allison.**

**1911 Indianapolis 500 entrant Ernest Delaney will finish 23rd.**

The *New York Times* reports on April 23, 1911 that the Indianapolis Motor Speedway is negotiating with Lloyds of London for a $10,000 insurance policy that would pay $100,000 if rain disrupts the running of the first 500.

This might be the first of thousands of courtesy vehicles available to the press over the last century.

This is Wild Will Jones' 1911 version of a full-face helmet.

Race cars are lined up four abreast to start the Indy 500 in 1911 and 1912, with the pace car on the inside of the pole car. In 1913, the pace car moves a few yards in front of the first row. The three-abreast lineup that remains in effect today begins in 1921.

Volunteers operated a clearinghouse where out-of-towners with no place to stay could hook up with locals with extra room. Restaurants ran out of food, ordered more, and ran out of that. Overcrowded hotels placed cots in the hallways. Nine hundred people were booked at the Claypool Hotel. For $1, a visitor could rent a chair for a few hours. In Shelbyville, 30 miles southeast, every hotel was filled.

Despite the best efforts of city police, it was gridlock on downtown streets. Within the mile square, hardly anything moved, which was a good thing, since the only sleep many people got was in their automobiles.

As dawn broke, the first of 15 special trains arrived. They brought an estimated 12,000 people from such cities as Chicago, Peoria and Springfield, Illinois; St. Louis and Cincinnati. Twelve interurban lines were depositing another 2,400 people an hour into the traction terminal.

In 1911, the Stoddard-Dayton passenger car, far right, lines up alongside the first row of racers, not out in front, and stays in that position during the "pace" lap. In a couple of years, the pace car is positioned ahead of the first row of racers.

5-30-11
500 Mile Race

The leader board at upper right shows eventual 1911 winner Ray Harroun in second place at the 170-mile mark.

The Big Four Railroad started running trains to the track at 4:30 a.m.; a full load was 1,100 people. Until 8 a.m., they ran every half-hour, then it was every 10 minutes. By noon, 38,000 people had made the 15-minute trip. The interurban line to the track proved ineffectual. It only managed to run three cars an hour on race day morning.

If the situation downtown was hectic, the scene around the Speedway was pure bedlam. In the three years since the track was carved out of the countryside, Marvel's general store had opened catty-corner across the Crawfordsville Pike from the Ben Hur waiting station. Georgetown Road along the western edge of the track had been graveled, but otherwise, the area was still mostly dirt roads and farmland.

The track had already hosted big crowds, so the locals knew what to expect. But this crowd was bigger by a long shot. Thousands of automobiles and a few horse-drawn carriages crowded the roads and country lanes for miles around. Ten thousand infield parking spots were soon filled.

Carl Fisher doubles the size of the purse. At $50,000 plus contingency awards, the 500 becomes the highest-paying sporting event anywhere in 1912. If it wasn't already, the Speedway is now the undisputed Taj Mahal of motorsport and the Indianapolis 500-Mile Sweepstakes is the world's most consequential automotive speed contest.

**When another car swerves to miss a riding mechanic who had fallen on the track, it crashed into Herbert Lytle's No. 35 Apperson, which is parked in its pit stall. He is out of the 1911 race.**

All 33,000 reserved seats were long gone at $1.50 apiece. So people bought $1 general admission tickets and swarmed into the remaining grandstands. When they were filled, crowds either began lining the field fencing on both sides of the track or people bought special tickets permitting them to watch the action from their parked cars.

Although some estimates had the crowd at 100,000, a number in the 80,000 range seems more plausible.

Regardless, at 10 a.m., Fisher appeared ceremoniously at the starting line wearing a white suit and driving a Stoddard-Dayton roadster. He motored away with 40 snarling racecars, now wrapped in heavy smoke and the smell of benzene and castor oil, tagging along at a sedate 40 miles an hour behind him. It was the first known rolling start of a major auto race and the first use of a pace car.

Carl brought the field down the long front straightaway. He pealed to the left near the starting line. Standing trackside, "Pop" Wagner waved his red flag. Thunder filled the air. And the first Indianapolis 500 was underway.

Of the 40 starters, only 12 actually ran the full 200 laps. Despite dire predictions of wholesale carnage, only one fatality occurred: Sam Dickson, a mechanic riding with Arthur Greiner, lost his life when Greiner's car hit the wall in the Southeast turn.

**Here's what's left of Harry Knight's Westcott after the pit area crash that took out Herbert Lytle's Apperson in 1911.**

Ray Harroun, the quiet little Marmon Co. engineer who had won two shorter Speedway events in 1910 and then quit racing, came out of retirement to hustle his yellow and black #32 "Wasp"—now equipped with the first known rear view mirror on an automobile—to a popular win. An episode during the race that had scorers scurrying to avoid an errant racecar left several lap times in question.

Whether or not genial Ralph Mulford, who had a faster car but needed many more pit stops to replace worn tires, was in the lead at the end, history books will forever show Harroun and relief driver Cyrus Patschke as winning the first 500-mile race at the Speedway.

While officials struggled all night to resolve the scoring snafu, Carl and Jane were entertaining jubilant guests at Blossom Heath, their home

Among the *what-ifs* that make history so interesting is this: Had Ralph Mulford been awarded the 1911 Indy victory, Ray Harroun's iconic little Marmon would be displaced as the winning car. Instead, the honor would go to a frumpy Lozier passenger car with its headlights and fenders removed. Mulford drove the Lozier down from Detroit before the race and drove back afterward. With its fender and lights reinstalled, it was sold as a used car.

Looking to the northwest, pit boxes in 1912 are covered by awnings.

on "Millionaire's Row" near White River about four miles northeast of the track. One more time, Carl had found the silver lining in the clouds.

Which is not to say the race was met with universal acclaim. The next day *The Indianapolis News* declared in its lead editorial that "Interesting and thrilling as was the race at the speedway yesterday, it is to be hoped that we have seen the last of these five-hundred-mile contests."

*The News* said since most of the entries were purpose-built racers, the event wasn't necessary for the improvement of production automobiles. "So the contest must be considered, not as a practical commercial test, but as a sport. And thus considered, we feel that it must be condemned in the extreme form which it took..."

But Fisher and his partners weren't fazed. They were already planning for 1912.

Soon, they announced a doubling of the prize fund. (It would rise to $55,875 by race time.) Then, they ordered a tunnel constructed beneath the Southeast turn to replace a bridge.

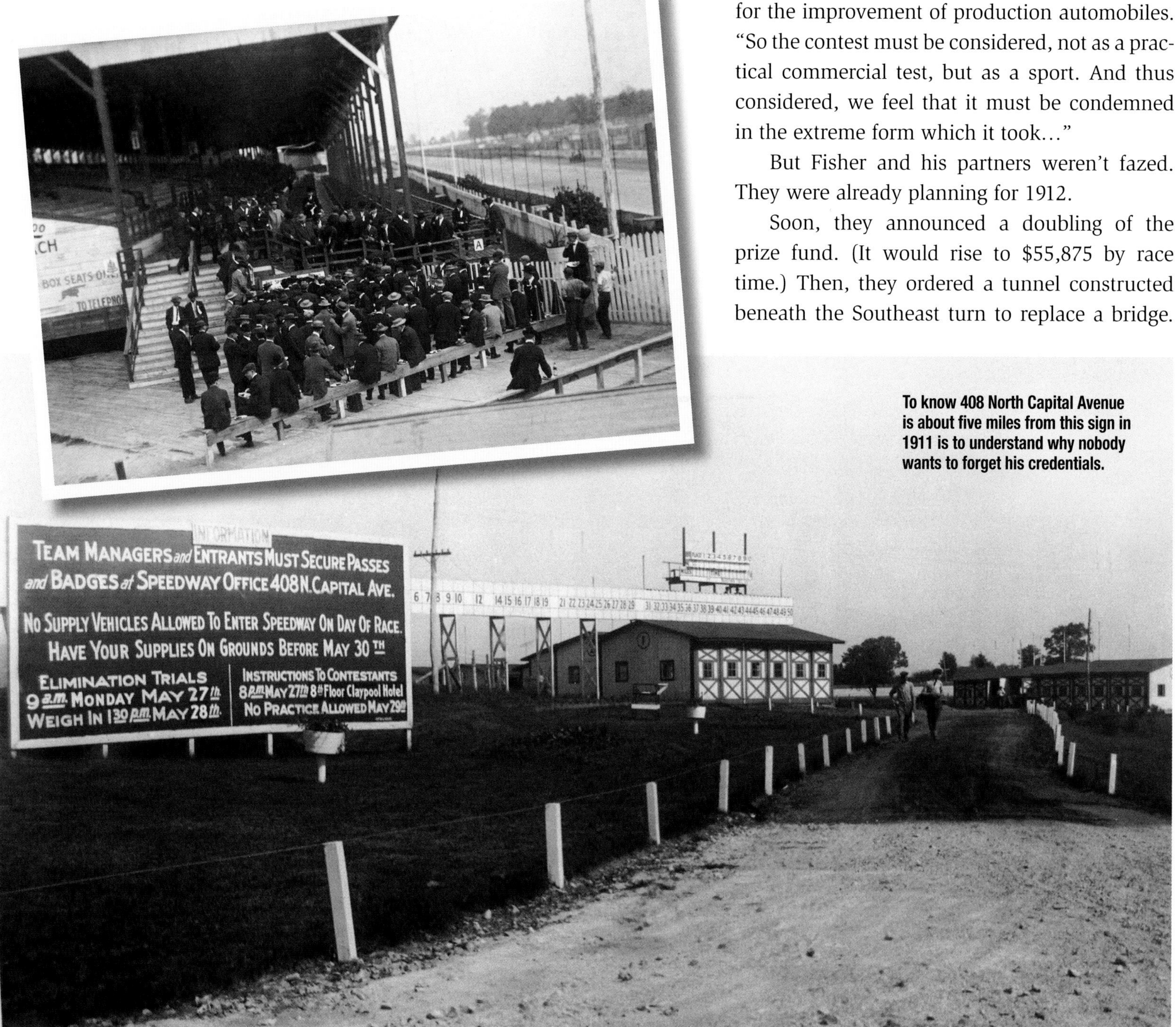


**An important meeting is about to take place in the grandstand near the entrance of Turn 1.**

**To know 408 North Capital Avenue is about five miles from this sign in 1911 is to understand why nobody wants to forget his credentials.**

And they raised ticket prices. General admission was still $1, but tickets to VIP seating areas cost a lot more. The box seats at the starting line: $10.

Bowing to an American Automobile Association edict (the AAA contest board was sanctioning the race) Fisher agreed to limit the field to 30 cars. Actually, only 27 started.

In one of the 500's most dramatic moments, highly regarded driver named Ralph DePalma was within a lap and a half of winning when his Mercedes quit.

While he and his mechanic, Rupert Jeffkins, were pushing the car down the main straightaway, a local boy named Joe Dawson made up a

**In the old days, the only thing separating the pit area from the track itself is a dim white line. The driver of the No. 16 car in this 1912 photo is Eddie Rickenbacker.**

two-lap deficit and sped to victory. DePalma had led 196 of the race's 200 laps.

Al Bloemker painted this picture in his book *500 Miles to Go:* "DePalma, head down and eyes on the ground, a picture of complete dejection, could hear the victory cheers. Nine cars were still running, and DePalma kept the big Mercedes close to the inside of the track. Jeffkins was at the tail, pushing with both hands. DePalma walked alongside the car, pushing with his right hand and steering with his left as they came into view of the spectators.

"Only a few noticed them at first. But a steadily increasing murmur swept through the stands. It grew into a cheering roar. DePalma raised his head and acknowledged the ovation with a wave of his right hand. Then, body erect, chin out, and a smile on is face, he paced off the remaining 600 yards to win acclaim as one of the most famous losers of all time."

A picture made the papers worldwide. It bolstered a growing notion of the Speedway as a deliciously unforgiving arena where nothing can be taken for granted and nobody is immune from calamity. Hardly three years since it was planted on the old Pressley farm, it already had a persona. It was becoming a brand.

DePalma would become even more famous as a winner of the 1915 500. His record for most laps led (612) over a racing career that spanned three decades stood for almost 70 years. But when serious students of the ancient history of the Speedway reminisce about the track's awful

**Drivers are in their cars, but Carl Fisher has not yet climbed into a Stutz A series he will use to pace the start of the 1912 race.**

By 1912, mechanization has impacted the track maintenance picture, but long wagon tongues suggest horses are still in the wings.

Accessory tents are lined up behind the pit area for the 1912 race. Notice the tall "aerodrome" in the background.

capacity for turning dreams into nightmares, they speak first of DePalma.

Fisher and his partners were ecstatic with almost everything about the 1912 race. That night at Blossom Heath, they talked about how to top it in 1913.

But Carl was soon to be distracted. There was the pending sale of Prest-O-Lite, which would make him a millionaire many times over. Then, he had a notion about tying together a string of state roads into a proper coast-to-coast thoroughfare he wanted to call the "Lincoln Highway." And on top of all that, he and Jane needed to check out a winter home he'd recently bought sight-unseen in Miami.

They were in Florida a couple of weeks after the race, and that's where Carl hooked up with an old man named John Collins.

Collins had run short on money trying to build a bridge in the bay between the little city of Miami and a 3,000-acre mangrove patch a short distance offshore. Shortly, Fisher owned 260 acres of mangrove swamp and Collins had $50,000 with which to finish the bridge.

The Speedway had consumed Carl for the last five years. He had obsessed over even the tiniest detail as he nurtured the

Covered in oil and grime, Joe Dawson's riding mechanic, Harry Martin, leans against their 1912 Indy winner.

A panoramic view outside Turn 1 in 1911.

facility through its infancy. Now, he had another world to conquer. He would rip out the mangroves, turn the swamp into an island with sand from the bay, and build the city of Miami Beach. After his death in 1939, there was a monument dedicated to him on the island. "He carved a great city from a jungle," it said.

Back in Indianapolis, he was content after the 1912 race to turn over more and more of the Speedway's heavy lifting to Allison and the staff, which consisted mainly of "Pop" Myers and "Dolly" Dallenbach.

**Racer attire varies greatly in the early days. Joe Dawson wears what amounts to a rain suit in 1912.**

**A car shares an infield driveway with a horse-drawn van in this 1912 photo.**

# Oldest Speedway Tradition Leaves Treasured Memories

Primitive lubricating systems mean racers dump clouds of oil on the bricks. The average car spews a quart every 10 miles. Assuming a third of the cars go the distance, upwards of 150 gallons of oil have made the track as slick as an ice skating rink by the time the race is over in 1913.

One hundred years ago, John Otte's great grandfather had a farm on Eagle Creek about a mile from the monster Speedway then beginning to reshape the landscape west of Indianapolis.

Some of the workmen who were hurriedly recruited to brick the track were lodged there.

Fast-forwarding a century, John Otte is the town of Speedway's retired fire chief. He chuckles at the thought that anyone might have paused back then to declare, "Hey, we're starting a tradition." But one got launched, nevertheless.

Opening their homes to out-of-towners, and their yards to their cars, is what Speedway residents have done since 1909. And what they still do.

The track was there first, of course. Lemon H. Trotter, who put the land deal together for Carl Fisher, subdivided some land to the southwest a couple of years later. He called it Speedway City, but it would not be incorporated until 1926.

The Trotter plan featured a wide main street running south from the Crawfordsville Pike with industry on the east and housing west. Residential lots started at $10 down and $10 a month.

The track loomed in the northeast like an immense fortress. Pop Myers lived on the premises, and a few people worked there, but except for those busy weekends in May, it didn't much affect daily life.

Even through the roaring '20s, race people and townspeople largely stayed out of each other's way. The money made from parking upwards of 25,000 cars once a year seemed an appropriate pay-back for the inconvenience the race caused the locals.

The Great Depression changed things. Residents looking to make ends meet and a racing fraternity largely living hand-to-mouth saw mutual benefit in getting better acquainted. Old-timers remember Speedway families in the '30s renting out their basements and bedrooms for the month.

The practice really picked up in 1946, when the Indianapolis Chamber of Commerce solicited help from the locals in finding rooms for race people. Through the '60s, many drivers, their families and their crews, along with accessory company reps and all manner of supporting staffers, roomed in Speedway for at least the month of May.

Louise Burcope, who moved with her husband to Speedway in 1940, says there were always willing renters. Legendary engine builder Herb Porter stayed with her for awhile. So did four-time 500 winner A.J. Foyt.

From 1947 until they stopped taking renters in the mid-50s, the Burcopes never changed their prices. It was $10 per person per week.

Since the track was home base for most of the teams on the AAA Champ Car circuit, many race people arrived in May and stayed through September. Teams rented garages at the track or around town. They ate at Petrovich's on 16th Street down by the railroad tracks. They partied at the nearby Mates' White Front bar, where Thursday nights were devoted to showing 16mm racing films. When a good finish rewarded them with a little extra prize money, they splurged at the B&B night club a mile farther east on 16th.

John Otte remembers driver Freddie Agabashian, his wife Mabel and their kids staying with

The Rosner building, then and now: Built in 1914 at the corner of 16th Street and Main Steet in the town of Speedway, the structure is largely unchanged today. The home of Rosner's drug store through much of the mid-20th Century, it anchored the north end of a vibrant half-mile of shops and businesses. Race teams frequently rented the upstairs living quarters.

them for awhile. When they found a house to rent, a neighbor sent Clint and Kay Brawner over. Clint was chief mechanic for Blakely Oil. Pretty soon, the whole team moved in.

"This was about 1950," Otte remembers. "And the Blakely team was high-dollar. They had two cars. And they had two or three pickups painted to match. I was just a little kid. You can imagine I was pretty thrilled.

"Later, it became the Dean Van Lines team. And that's when Jimmy Bryan entered the picture."

Speedway historian Donald Davidson's write-up about the Otte family's relationship with Bryan is worth whatever you have to pay for a copy of the 1987 Indianapolis 500 yearbook.

"Jimmy Bryan was like a big brother to me," Otte says today. "Only more so. He was my hero."

For seven summers, Jimmy was in and out of the Otte house.

"Yes, the story about him lounging on the front yard after winning the 500 in '58 and us getting into a wrestling match is true," Otte says.

"He was still in his yellow Belond uniform. People were walking by on the way to their cars. I don't think anybody realized that here was the guy who had just won the 500."

John Otte was 16 in 1960. He was on a family outing in southern Indiana on Father's Day when the radio carried the news of Bryan's fatal crash at Langhorne, Pennsylvania.

"I still choke up when I think about it," he says now. "Mom and dad kept taking in race people after that, but no more drivers. We just couldn't do that anymore."

Jules Goux went so fast in 1913 he won by more than 13 minutes. His winning margin is a record that still stands.

It's not that Gil Anderson's Stutz is moving very fast in this 1913 photo; rather, the camera's shutter drops so slowly across the lens that the image is distorted. That's why the car appears to be leaning forward as it slips beneath the starter's bridge.

CHAPTER 6

# THRIVING AMID RECESSION AND WAR

If you have a suggestion about how to improve the Speedway's customer service, the sign urges you to write it down and leave it in that black box on the fence post in the foreground.

The track and the area around it got another facelift for the 1913 race. A five-story timing and scoring facility replaced two smaller structures. Located just a few feet from the inside edge of the track at the starting line, it looked so sufficiently of Japanese design and quickly became the "Pagoda."

Driver Jack Tower and mechanic Lee Dunning pose casually in their Mason after qualifying at 88 mph in 1913. Beneath the sheet metal, both engine and chassis are Duesenberg.

The original Pagoda, built for the 1913 race, is deliberately burned down 12 years later to make way for one further back from the tracks. The photo at right shows the structure under construction.

The elevated scoreboard just after the finish of the 1914 race. There's a lot of information.

Eddie Rickenbacker, 1914.

A second tunnel, this under the main straightaway, made the infield a little more accessible and a separate garage area for the European teams Fisher had invited materialized outside Turn 2, about where the Brickyard Crossing Inn is today.

The Prest-O-Lite plant was up and running, and a sliver of farmland to the west was about to become home to many workmen and their families. Fisher's personal real estate agent, Lemon Trotter, opened his Speedway Realty office and began advertising lots for sale. The price: $10 down and $10 a month.

Frenchman Jules Goux won the 1913 "500" in a Peugeot, consuming a little champagne on one or more of his pit stops and a bottle in victory lane.

Given the large expanse that is the Indianapolis Motor Speedway, Theodore Pilette appears to be getting his car refueled out in the country instead of in the infield in 1913.

Young Tony Hulman sees his first Indianapolis 500-Mile Race in 1914. He is 13 years old.

Tall grass chokes the inside of Turn 4, where Jean Chassagne flips his Sunbeam in 1914.

The 1914 program costs 10 cents.

Frenchman Rene Thomas, left, shows off his Delage car before winning the 1914 race.

The building boom continued into 1914. Two more big grandstands, one in the southwest turn and the other on the main straight, plus a catwalk 25 feet above the track at the starting line greeted the 1914 crowd. With Goux now leading a veritable European invasion, the French monopolized the race. They swept the first four places. Rene Thomas won it in a Delage. Fisher's old friend Barney Oldfield was fifth in a Stutz.

Al Bloemker says in his book, *500 Miles to Go,* the financial picture for Fisher and his partners was bright enough that a dividend was paid for the first time after the 1914 race, but there were economic and political clouds on the horizon.

On June 28, Austria's Archduke Ferdinand and his wife were shot and killed. War seemed imminent. Carl and Jane sailed for Paris, anyway; Jane to see the sights and Carl to beat the drums for

**Georges Boillot, left, seems to be in vigorous communication with Johnny Aitken before the 1914 race. Aitken, a retired driver who coached Joe Dawson to his 1912 Indy 500 victory, had been recruited by Carl Fisher to assist the French team. He is successful.**

**Barney Oldfield could often be found with his trademark cigar clenched in his teeth.**

**Smartly attired Dario Resta (there's a coat and tie under his duster) and his mechanic wear identical houndstooth caps in 1915.**

**The checkered flag waves from the bridge and 1915 winner Ralph DePalma hikes his arm in triumph. The inset photo shows early racing superstar Barney Oldfield with a Firestone logo on his personal car and a dandy squad of helpers.**

**The 1915 program at far right warns buyers not to pay more than a dime.**

more European entries. They were still there when war broke out. Jane would say later that their narrow escape from France on the last available ship was "The greatest race of Carl's career."

Back home, another grandstand, a third tunnel and 30 new garages were in place before the 1915 race. Although some of their machinery turned up at the Speedway, the European drivers did not.

# 500 FESTIVAL
## THE PARADE IS NOT THE HALF OF IT

Since it wasn't technically a Speedway function, Tony Hulman had not planned to participate in the first 500 Festival parade through downtown Indianapolis on May 29, 1957, and he certainly wasn't expecting what he saw.

Thirty minutes beforehand, Tony was still at the track tending to matters involving the next day's race, when Festival top-gun Howdy Wilcox, Jr. went looking for him.

Years later, Wilcox remembered it this way: "I said, 'Tony, you have got to be down there.' He said, 'You really think I do?' I said, 'You really haven't got any choice.' And I took him down myself."

Hulman found 150,000 people lining the parade route.

While it was said in the early days that the Speedway didn't really *need* the Festival, Tony's experience that night in '57 assured the future of a relationship that has grown through the years beyond the founders' wildest dreams.

500 Festival, Inc. is a non-profit mostly volunteer organization with just one purpose: to produce events and programs in support of the Indy 500.

The parade, a memorial service, a street dance and a black-tie ball got things rolling that night in '57. Soon, the entire month of May was sprinkled with Festival activities. There was the annual mayor's breakfast, the queen contest, gin rummy, bowling and golf tournaments, a mammoth mechanic recognition party, fashion shows. And, of course, the parade.

In 1976, word came from the Speedway that maybe a foot race or a bike race might be a nice addition to the Indy 500 weekend. Since a bike race would conflict with Indiana University's Little 500, a foot race it would be. Staged by a bank and the Fellowship of Christian Athletes in '77 and '78, the mini-marathon became a 500 Festival event in '79.

Moved to early May and capped now at 35,000 entries, the "mini" is the largest half-marathon in the United States.

In 2004, the 500 Festival joined the Speedway in an education program for fourth graders throughout Indiana. The first year saw about 5,000 students involved. More than 25,000 took part in 2008, many of them culminating their experience with a field trip to the track.

**Just a few of the more than 35,000 OneAmerica 500 Festival mini marathoners are on the main straight at the Speedway.**

**The 500 Festival parade salutes the first half-century of the Indy 500 as it moves through the streets of downtown Indianapolis in 1961.**

Many were in combat. Ralph DePalma, revered far and wide for his heroics in 1912, won this time although, in a situation reminiscent of his earlier loss, his engine broke a rod with three laps to go. This time he was able to nurse his car to victory lane.

With Europe engulfed in World War I and with U.S. car makers showing little interest in racing, the Fisher partners worried about the car count for 1916. They ended up buying two Peugeots and arranging with the Premier company in Indianapolis to build three just like them.

Fisher and Allison formed their own Prest-O-Lite team, obtained two Maxwells, and hired a journeyman race driver from Columbus, Ohio to run it. His name was Eddie Rickenbacker. In 10 years he would own the track.

**Driver Pete Henderson and his mechanic wear cloth hats for this official 1916 photo.**

**Right: Under their pristine white coveralls, Prest-O-Lite team members are decked out in white dress shirts and ties. That's none other than Eddie Rickenbacker third from the right. Carl Fisher and Jim Allison own the team.**

**Below: Race team members gather with the cars behind them in this 1916 wide-angle photo from the starting line.**

Rickenbacker was among the 21 drivers taking the green flag for the Indianapolis 300-mile race in 1916. He led the first 10 laps, but Dario Resta won it handily.

Fisher had shortened the event, not necessarily out of a concern for the war effort but because he had a hunch 500 miles was just a bit much. Rarely was Carl wrong on a hunch, but he was this time. The next long race at the Speedway would not be until Memorial Day, 1919, and the distance would be back to 500 miles.

Pretty sure the U.S. would be drawn into the Great War and that racing would be halted for the duration, Fisher proposed one last event in 1916—the September 8 Harvest Auto Racing Classic.

"We might be able to pick up a profit of $20,000 or more to tide us over," he said.

A big Labor Day weekend race at the new board track in Cincinnati had been especially hard on equipment, however, so the field was short the next week at Indianapolis. It would have been worse except that six of the 16 cars entered were Speedway property. They were unmolested and good to go. Only 10,000 spectators showed up,

This photo of Barney Oldfield getting new tires in 1916 reveals the track's uneven brick surface.

In only seven months at the end of World War I in 1918, Eddie Rickenbacker downs 22 German planes and four balloons. As America's "Ace of Aces," the war hero comes home to ticker tape parades.

The grille on the Premier pace car in 1916 is not stock, leading historians to speculate that the car might have been modified just for the race. That's Eddie Rickenbacker getting settled in Car 5.

Throwing a bone to his critics, Carl Fisher renames the 1919 race "Liberty Sweep Stakes" and moves it back a day from Memorial Day. This is the program. The official program in 1920, at far right, jumps in price to 15 cents.

Capt. Robert Hammond of the British Royal Flying Corps is killed in a plane crash at the Speedway in 1918. Carl Fisher has Hammond's ashes placed temporarily in space he has reserved for himself in a mausoleum at Crown Hill Cemetery. The ashes are still there.

Louis Chevrolet's brother Gaston (in goggles) and riding mechanic John Bresnahan, posing for a photo taken during practice, eventually win the 1920 race in this bullet-nosed Frontenac. The Chevrolets have seven cars in the race. Steering arm failures knock five out. Louis supposedly gave this car a post-race kick. And its steering arm fell off.

Everyone is ready for the start of the 1921 race except Roscoe Sarles, No. 6.

but the pay-off wasn't that bad. The Speedway cars won $5,900 of the $12,000 in prize money.

Even before America entered the war in 1917, Fisher had a plan to convert the infield into "the best damned flight school in the military." By late summer, hangers and runways were in place along with floodlights for night landings. The facility became a stopover on a training route from Dayton, Ohio to Rantoul, Illinois. In addition, an aviation maintenance battalion was stationed there.

More than 100 acres of tillable infield was turned back into cropland, and the partners received $3,698.50 from the Marmon Co., which used the track to check-ride 2,998 brand-new cars in the two years.

Maintenance expenses on the huge facility far outpaced income, however. As the bills piled up, Fisher proposed to the partners a special cash assessment of 60 percent of their holdings. That was okay with Art Newby and Jim Allison, but too much for Frank Wheeler, who sold his stock to Allison.

Five-year-old Ernest Eppen helped his dad park cars on the family's acreage across Georgetown Pike from the Speedway in 1919. For the next 67 years, Ernie's parking money augments income from the Eppen truck farm. All but a half-acre is sold to the Speedway in 1986, but Ernie still accommodates a few cars through the 2003 race.

**Louis Fontaine had a bad day in his Miller Junior 18 in 1921, his only race.**

This is one of the first known aerial photos of the Speedway on a race day. It's 1922. A few residents along Georgetown Road are parking cars in their yards. Notice the vast amount of open farmland to the west.

Jimmy Murphy.

Prior to the 500 in 1922, driver Jimmy Murphy is made an honorary Indian Chief and presented with a headdress by Yellow Calf, a full-blooded Arapahoe. Murphy proceeds to win the race.

The cars look fine before the five-plus-hour race grind begins in 1922. That's Jimmy Murphy's Miller-powered Duesenberg, No. 35, on the pole. He wins.

The four-man Speedway owner's club was down to three, but at least the facility was solvent.

Just six months after Armistice Day, the Speedway was spruced up and awaiting the 1919 500, and the sound of airplanes was about to be replaced by the sound of race engines. Not everybody was happy about that. Ten years after racecars first enveloped the old Pressley farm in smoke and thunder, a segment of Indianapolis society yearned for peace and quiet. What went on out there west of town was labeled by the upper crust as a "vulgar spectacle."

*The Indianapolis News* thought the idea of a race on Memorial Day was "a rank desecration of a national holiday." To assuage the critics and to

**The DePalma brothers, John, left, and Ralph, right, wear ties as they meet with fellow driver Cliff Durant in 1923.**

**That's an oil-soaked Tommy Milton seated (with drinking glass) on the back of his No. 2 Frontenac after winning the 1921 race. The two fellows to his left are car owner Louis Chevrolet, in the straw hat, and Eddie Edenburn. Arthur Chevrolet is directly behind him.**

**A British citizen whose mother was American and father a Polish count, Louis Zborowski drives in the 1923 race. He finishes 20th in a Bugatti.**

**A Roman gladiator graces the cover of the 1924 program.**

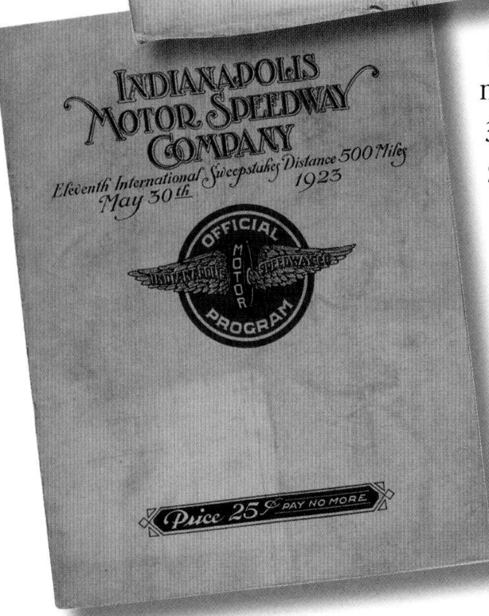


**Bland is back for a program cover in 1923, but the price now is a quarter.**

gain the benefit of a weekend crowd, Fisher moved the event back a day to Saturday, May 31. Then he changed the name to "Liberty Sweepstakes," raised the purse to $50,000, appointed Eddie Rickenbacker, now a war hero, as the referee, and sent people far and wide in search of enough rolling stock to fill the field.

Of course, the Speedway cars, which had been crucial to the success of the 1915 and 1916 races, weren't hard to find. They were stabled across the street. Allison had constructed an engineering shop in the development Lemon Trotter was promoting as Speedway City.

Like an oak from an acorn, the shop would grow exponentially. General Motors bought it in 1929 and it became the Allison Division of General Motors.

Somehow, Fisher got his full field of 33 cars. Howdy Wilcox II took the checkered flag while a trackside band was playing a new song then making the rounds in Indianapolis, which eventually became known for the opening line of its refrain: "Back Home Again in Indiana." Opera star James Melton sang it for the first time at the 1946 "500." It remains today a Speedway tradition.

The early 1920s saw the House of Chevrolet reigning at the Speedway. Brothers Louis, Art and Gaston fielded seven cars in the 1920 race. They were highly modified bullet-nosed Model T Fords with jewel-like engines of Chevrolet design.

**There's a lot to see in this 1920s image of photographers and their gear at the Speedway. That's a Stutz they're leaning on. One cameraman has a flash unit. Note the press credentials on a few hats.**

**Tommy Milton in the 1920 Duesenberg.**

Ten years after the first 500, when almost every car was a stripped version of a production automobile and likely driven by an employee of the carmaker that built it, mainstream manufacturers are gone by 1921. To be competitive now you need a special-built Duesenberg or one of those lightweight Frontenac racers. Soon, you'd need a Miller.

Gaston ended up winning the race without having to change a single one of his Firestone tires. It so happened that every 500 winner for the better part of five decades after that would run on Firestones.

Louis and Art were back in 1921, but without Gaston, who had perished in a California racing accident in November. The brothers had two cars. Tommy Milton, who would become one of the Speedway's all-time greatest drivers, piloted one of them to victory lane.

But machinery from the shops of Augie and Fred Duesenberg and Harry Miller dominated racing for the rest of the decade. The era of the purposed-built racer had arrived. A Duesenberg was second in 1921. Seven of the first eight were Duesenbergs in 1922.

The car Milton won with in 1923 was called an HSC, which stood for the Harry Stutz Company, but it was a Miller in every way but name.

Duesenbergs came in first and sixth in 1924, but there were 11 Millers in the top 13.

Duesenbergs won again in 1925 and 1927. It was a Miller parade to victory lane through the rest of the roaring '20s.

Some years all but four or five cars out of the 33 taking the green flag were Millers. Miller engines would morph into the Offenhausers and later the Meyer-Drakes that ruled Indianapolis until the mid-1960s.

Fisher had hired an energetic United Press wire service reporter named Steve Hannagan before the 1920 race to handle Speedway promotion. It was a stroke of genius. Steve and Carl shared a

# Blame It on...Radio

If one word could explain America's early infatuation with the Indianapolis Motor Speedway and the Indy 500, it might be radio.

Query old-timers about their earliest memories of the big Indy race, and almost to a person they will talk about radio. They heard it first on the radio. Many remember exactly where they were year to year, which wasn't that difficult since the same ritual occurred year to year. People gathered around the kitchen table or on the porch or in the back yard. It was Memorial Day, a national holiday. But it was also Race Day. The kids knew the drill: shush so the adults could hear.

Radio broadcaster Sid Collins interviews driver Jimmy Reece in 1958.

But enough of the youngsters vowed to one day see a 500 in person that ever larger Speedway crowds were assured.

By some accounts, the first live race reports from the track occurred in 1922. WGN's A.J. Kaney was reporting from the Speedway in 1924. WFBM in Indianapolis carried live reports in 1925.

NBC's famous Graham McNamee, who had called the Dempsey/Tunney heavyweight fight, the World Series and the 1924 GOP national convention, built a 30-minute show around the finish of the 1928 race and several others thereafter.

Ted Husing filed reports for CBS in the late 1930s. Using Cincinnati's WLW to originate, the Mutual Network also carried the race through 1941.

Sid Collins began his race day reports with Indy's own WIBC in 1948. Collins and his crew stayed on in 1952, when the Speedway formed its own network.

To spread the action around, announcers from all four Indianapolis AM stations formed the team to call the 1953 race, and every station carried it live flag to flag. The Armed Forces network also came aboard in '53. Worldwide station count in the early 1970s was over 1,200.

Collins was chief announcer until his death in 1977. Paul Page was chief through the 1987 race. Lou Palmer did the honors in '88 and '89. Bob Jenkins was at the helm through '98, when he passed the mic to Mike King.

sixth sense about how to tickle the public fancy.

Take the matter of attendance figures. From the very beginning, precise numbers were never revealed and that left the door open to all manner of speculation. Hannagan played the issue like a violin. Were there 50,000 people on the grounds? Or 150,000? Or 250,000? Hannagan's way of responding tended to support ever-higher guesses, which fed a bigger-than-life perception of the Speedway and the events it hosted.

In a career that spanned 30 years, the native of Lafayette, Indiana, helped Carl put Miami Beach and Montauk Point, Long Island, on the map, covered the celebrity beat as a United Press writer in New York, and orchestrated the elevation of Sun Valley and Las Vegas into household words.

**Drivers, mechanics and car owners gather for the obligatory panoramic group photo prior to the start of the 1924 Indy 500.**

Infield parking behind the pits puts these VIPs within a few feet of the action. Ladies and gentlemen stand on their cars to better see the start of the 1925 race.

CHAPTER 7

# RICKENBACKER TAKES CHARGE

**Eddie Rickenbacker.** *U.S. Air Force*

Students of the Fisher era in Speedway history mostly agree something happened in the run-up to the 1923 race that took the fun out of it for Carl.

That was the year after a bill made it through the Indiana General Assembly outlawing "commercial sports" on Memorial Day. Governor Warren McCray vetoed the measure, but the strength of sentiment against the race left Carl greatly distressed.

He circulated word right afterward that since the track had outlived its original purpose, he'd be willing to sell it.

"The Speedway's original purpose was for experimental work intended to improve the automobile," he said. "Interest displayed in the 500-mile race as a sport attraction definitely has been regarded by some as of secondary importance, and as such, does not deserve serious consideration now."

The bluff had the desired effect. People from all walks of life, from auto industry VIPS like Henry Ford on down, let him know they valued the facility and the race.

**The 1925 program color is yellow with a bald eagle as the cover feature.**

**VIP parking in back of the pits is very tight in 1925, but you get to watch the race from the top of your car.**

Nevertheless, on June 11, 1923, just 15 years after his monster racetrack was carved out of the old Pressley farm, Fisher stepped aside as president of the Speedway company, and Jim Allison took over. Although by some accounts, he sold his stock at the same time, it's clear Fisher was still in on the decision-making in 1926, when the track was put on the market again.

This time, nobody was bluffing.

On August 15, 1927, Eddie Rickenbacker, the poor kid from Columbus who first raced in the 500 in 1912 and the WW I hero who would one day found Eastern Airlines, became only the second owner of the Indianapolis Motor Speedway.

Actually, Rickenbacker was the front man for a small group of wealthy Detroiters. Their identities remain unknown to this day, but they paid for the place with cash and 6.5 percent mortgage bonds totaling $700,000.

Not much else was revealed about the transaction. But the stated sale price is so small—and the deal-making deftness of the Fisher team so large—it's easy to surmise that there were other considerations. Surely, the monster edifice went for more than a couple thousand dollars an acre.

Pop Myers and Dolly Dallenbach stayed on to run the place for Rickenbacker, and Fisher and Allison joined the board of directors. Fisher

**Reserved trackside parking is the cat's meow in 1929, but you still must fight the traffic in and out of the infield.**

stayed tuned for several more years to what was happening at the Speedway and in auto racing generally. As late as 1935, Carl and Rickenbacker were talking about building a massive Indianapolis-style track in South Florida.

Of the four founders, Frank Wheeler had taken his own life in 1921, and pneumonia claimed Allison in 1928. Art Newby died in 1933. Carl Fisher died while undergoing treatment for sclerosis of the liver in 1939.

His fortune, estimated at $100 million in the mid-'20s, had evaporated. A 1925 hurricane wiped out Miami Beach and he mothballed the Montauk Point project and redirected his resources into south Florida. Then, he watched it all drain away as the Great Depression killed the market for high-dollar winter havens on the tropical island he had dredged from the sea. "I've become a beggar-man," he told a friend a few days before his death.

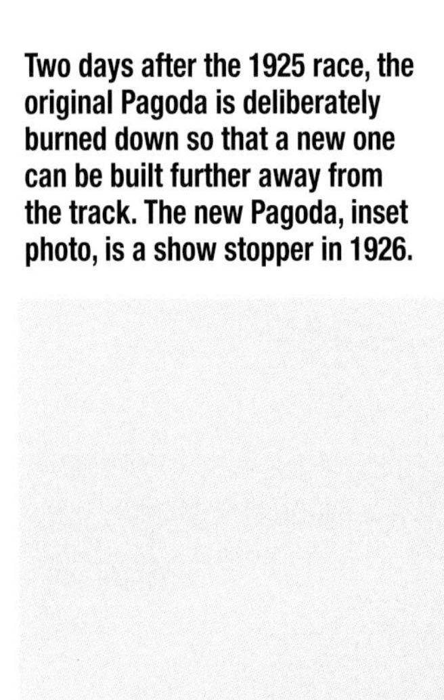

**Two days after the 1925 race, the original Pagoda is deliberately burned down so that a new one can be built further away from the track. The new Pagoda, inset photo, is a show stopper in 1926.**

Meanwhile at the Speedway, aside from a new grandstand between turns one and two and a new Pagoda farther back from the track than the first one, not much changed from 1915 to the late '20s.

One of the first major construction projects Rickenbacker undertook did not involve the track or the grandstands. Rather, it was a golf course. He commissioned local architect William Diddle to lay out the course on much of the infield and some property outside the track to the east. Within a year, it was complete: nine holes inside the track and nine outside. Another nine holes eventually were constructed outside the track; a total makeover in the early 1990s left 14 holes outside and four inside.

With its transmission cover removed, the jewel-like design of one of Harry Miller's front-wheel-drive creations becomes even more apparent. That radiator mesh is soldered in place wire by wire. Check out the inboard brakes. No wonder Miller was such a dominant force in the '20s.

Frank Lockhart.

Frank Lockhart perishes on April 25, 1928 during a speed run on the beach at Daytona. The car he has prepared for the upcoming Indy 500 is assigned to Ray Keech, who finishes fourth. Keech is back in Lockhart's car for the 1929 race, which he wins.

Frank Lockhart, shown here in 1927, became an instant star in 1926 when he won as a rookie.

**Louis Schwitzer, who won the Speedway's first automobile race in 1909, is a highly regarded AAA official in the 1920s. An annual engineering achievement award given in his name remains to this day one of the most coveted prizes in motorsport.**

**Louis Meyer becomes a rookie winner in 1928, and wins two more races in the 1930s.**

Louis Meyer, whose only previous experience at Indianapolis is the 41 laps he subbed for Wilbur Shaw in 1927, wins the first of his three Indy 500s in 1928. For the next 50 years, Louis would work his magic at the Speedway as a mechanic, driver and engine builder.

Rickenbacker saw the course as revenue source, but it was more than that. Since 1911, the Speedway was off limits to ordinary mortals except for a few weeks in May. Surrounded by high board fences and barbed wire, it was a foreboding place.

The golf course made the facility a little friendlier. People would play it just to say they had actually been inside the Speedway.

The Speedway might have been a little shabby when Eddie Rickenbacker took over on August 15, 1927, but there was a bigger problem.

The 500-mile race was becoming a playground for Harry Miller, the engine wizard extraordinaire whose work was so good he was hurting the show. Racing historian Griffith Borgeson called Miller in 1998 the "greatest creative figure in the history of the American racing car."

In the decade of the '20s, sophisticated Miller engines, then entire cars, were the dominant

The Duesenberg brothers, Augie, left, and Fred, build sturdy, luxurious cars in the 1920s.

New garages are built in 1929.

It's 1928 and those trees in the north end constitute the picnic grove, where many a race fan will lunch and nap before the five-hour race is history.

**A 1930 aerial photo emphasizes the rectangular shape of the track.**

**Speedway aerial view.**

The town of Speedway is incorporated on July 14, 1926, 12 years after Lemon Trotter began selling lots in a development he called Speedway City, and 17 years after the Indianapolis Motor Speedway is built. There are 67 property owners and 507 residents at the time.

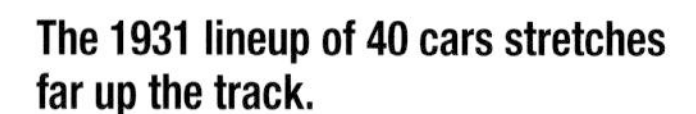

**The 1931 lineup of 40 cars stretches far up the track.**

force at the Brickyard. From 1923 through 1928, 83 percent of the entries were Millers. Only the supercharged Duesenbergs were their equals, and there weren't many of them.

The dynasty had actually begun in 1922, when young Jimmy Murphy swapped the engine in his Duesenberg with a Miller and won the race.

Tommy Milton backed it up with a win the following year in an H.S.C., which was all Miller under the skin.

Using a mysterious power-boosting fuel additive called tetraethyl lead, Milton had his engine set to run at an unheard-of 7.5:1 compression ratio. He gained maybe 10 percent more horsepower, but that was enough. After that, everybody wanted a Miller and a little jar of "Ethyl." Although highly toxic, the elixir would soon make its way into gasoline stocks world wide, and revolutionize passenger car engine design.

Duesenbergs won the 500 in 1924 and 1925, but there were packs of Millers behind them: 13 of the top 15 in '24, 15 of the top 20 in '25.

It rained in 1926, (the race was halted at 400 miles) which well-suited Frank Lockhart, a free-spirited California kid with absolutely no experience at Indianapolis. He electrified the crowd as he finessed a Miller to victory.

At the 50-mile mark, here's a look at the scoreboard in 1931.

**This photo of Wilbur Shaw going over the wall in 1931 got big play worldwide. Shaw's car was "touched up" in the photo and therefore looks superimposed, but that's really him.**

At least eight spectators have found perches in this bedraggled tree in 1931.

The huge Wheeler-Shebler Trophy is retired after the 1932 race. Shown here is the winning team. From left: that's riding mechanic Jerry Houck, driver Fred Frame, car owner Harry Hartz and chief mechanic Jean Marcenac.

To encourage production car testing at the track, Samuel Stevens of Rome, New York, underwrites the creation of the Stevens Trophy in 1927. It's for the best 24-hour performance by a regulation passenger sedan at an average speed of more than 60 mph. The first winner is a Stutz, which averages 68.44 mph while covering 1,642.58 miles in early April.

Lockhart was on his way to a repeat in 1927 when his Miller lost a connecting rod. George Souders won in a Duesenberg, but of the 33 starters, 28 were Miller-powered.

Such was the scene confronting Rickenbacker as he picked up the reins at the Speedway. Purpose-built racing machinery had long since erased the notion of the track as a passenger car proving ground. Now, the 500 was taking a step further: it was becoming an exclusive one-marquee parade.

The car count was on the decline. Tickets were getting a little harder to sell. Something had to be done.

The contest board of the AAA wrote the rulebook for the Indianapolis 500 and for many other events, including the dozen or so on the so-called "Champ Car" circuit, of which Indy was the crown jewel. Everybody was feeling the pinch.

Since Rickenbacker was also the chairman of the contest board, there were no major disagreements about what to do. A rules change designed to encourage more diverse entries, drastically cut costs, and make racecars more closely resemble street cars, was soon announced.

A drum and bugle corps marches smartly down the track on race morning in 1932.

It's 1932, and farm trucks are pressed into service as mobile viewing platforms. Two young ladies wearing dresses and high heels seem ready to climb aboard.

Rules changes encouraging stock-block engines entice a few factories back to the Speedway in the early 1930s. Here's the Studebaker team in 1932. All five cars make the race. They finish third, sixth, 13th, 15th and 16th.

**This infield refreshment stand collects a crowd in 1933. Signs advertise 32-cent beer. Cokes are 10 cents.**

**That's a star-struck Florsheim salesman on the left watching as Wilbur Shaw, Louis Meyer, white hat, rear, and Lou Moore, right, try on some new shoes in 1933. Even for top-gun racers, money is tight and promotional opportunities like this very scarce. No wonder the boys look happy.**

Tony Hulman plays end on Yale University's undefeated football team in 1924. He had made the all-America scholastic track team in 1919 (high hurdles) and 1920 (pole vault).

Whereas the tiny thoroughbred race engines of the late '20s were exquisitely crafted and very expensive, the new rules permitted low-cost, low-tech "stock-block" engines of up to 366 cubic inches. For awhile, at least, superchargers and four-valve cylinder heads were out. Two-man cars were back in.

The new formula wouldn't take effect at Indianapolis until 1930, leaving the Millers to continue their winning streak in both 1928 and 1929.

Pundits predicted that would be end of it, however, for exotic full-race machinery.

They were only partly right.

It was pure coincidence that the so-called "junk formula" was applied in 1930—a few months after the stock market crash. But the timing couldn't have been better. As the economy deflated, even wealthy sportsmen had second thoughts about spending $15,000 for a purpose-built racer when a $1,500 modified production car could make the same show.

With many small adjustments along the way, the formula was in effect through 1937. It democratized the racing industry. The little guy was back. The 1931 entry list contained 70 names, double the number of two years earlier.

The variety was a sight to see. In 1931, for example, a Duesenberg powered by a Cummins

**Here's a high-powered group gathered around an unidentified radio announcer. Among the VIPs: Eddie Rickenbacker, boat builder Gar Wood and chief steward Eddie Edenburn.**

**Newsreel cameramen with their bulky equipment film the 1933 race.**

**Push cars built to look like their big brothers are ready to race in 1934.**

**Speedway corner reconstruction.**

Unless the original bricks are damaged, they are reused after the corners are reconstructed in 1935.

**The AAA's Eric Von Hombach with his official 1935 Ford.**

diesel went the full 500 miles without a pit stop, and did it on $2.55 in fuel.

Low-priced custom car builders took so much business away from Harry Miller that he was soon nearly bankrupt.

And wonder of wonders, some big factory teams tried their luck. Studebaker was in with five cars in 1933. That was the year Rickenbacker faced down a driver rebellion over Howdy Wilcox II. Howdy was a well-respected driver who had diabetes. Several hours before race time, the resident Speedway physician pronounced him unfit to drive.

A one-sentence petition quickly materialized, which every driver signed. They wouldn't participate in the 500 unless Howdy was allowed back in. Wilbur Shaw was among them. Shaw said in his book, *Gentlemen, Start Your Engines*, that track officials met with everybody about 15

**Speedway general manager Pop Myers is surrounded by budding race drivers during a kid's pushmobile race in the 1930s; notice the various uniform styles. Below are kids in cars poised for a standing start.** *Junior Dryer collection*

**This early morning photo shows a pre-race scene along pit row in 1937.**

**Cliff Bergere.**

Cliff Bergere works out on his make-shift steering apparatus. Strong-arming an early racecar around the Speedway for 500 miles requires muscle.

minutes before the green flag was supposed to fall. The meeting was still going 25 minutes later when Rickenbacker, who knew a little something about pressure situations, ended the argument.

"...This race is going to start in exactly five minutes if there is only one car ready to run at that time and I have to drive it myself," he said.

Shaw noted that the green flag waved at 10:15 to a full field. The Wilcox car started at the back with Mauri Rose driving.

The year 1935 saw another big carmaker take on Indy. The Ford Motor Co. paid Harry Miller a reported $200,000 to build five cars along with five back-ups. Four qualified. They bristled with technical innovations, but Miller had located a delicate steering gear too close to the engine block.

When the heat made the grease boil off, the gear "froze." With a greatly distressed Henry Ford and an entourage of Ford executives looking on, the cars fell by the wayside one by one. Not a single Ford was running at the end. It would be almost 30 years before factory Ford machinery raced again at the Speedway.

But Rickenbacker had himself a pretty good show, anyway. Despite worsening track conditions and low-tech hardware, speeds actually increased in the 1930s. The pole speed in 1929 was about 115 mph. In 1936, it was 119.6.

The new formula was supposed to favor stock-block engines, but it's a fact that race-bred Millers, redesigned per the new rules, kept their winning streak going through 1935.

That's when a shirttail descendent of the Miller called the Offenhauser burst upon the scene. Offy engines would dominate the Brickyard for the next 30 years.

Taking the lineup photo in 1929.

CHAPTER 8

# HARD TIMES AND WAR

The Indy 500 celebrates its 15th birthday in 1927. It's the last race for the Fisher group.

Speedway senior executives, from left: Chester Ricker, Pop Myers, Charlie Merz and Eddie Rickenbacker.

Maybe it was an escape, an opportunity to forget for a day the grinding reality of the Great Depression. But race day in the 1930s found tens of thousands invading the Speedway and millions more crowding around radio sets on the nation's kitchen tables and front porches to listen to the Indianapolis 500.

It's what America did on Memorial Day.

But the Speedway was not immune from economic woe. Eddie Rickenbacker was pinching pennies, too. Unlike Carl Fisher before him and Tony Hulman afterward, Rickenbacker couldn't plow big money into track maintenance. He had stockholders to answer to, and they expected a return on their investment.

Moreover, Rickenbacker had a lot on his mind. On January 1, 1935, he moved to New York and took over the day-to-day operations of Eastern Airlines.

Pop Myers had a free hand at the Speedway, but Rickenbacker watched over the checkbook.

Upkeep lagged. The concrete walls, some dating back to 1909,

A toy wagon hauls starter batteries as a mechanic works on the Cummins Diesel in 1931.

That's the renowned Chester Ricker on the right, the Speedway's director of timing and scoring from 1913 to 1951. His system used a ship's chronometer to drive a Stewart-Warner timer.

were sinking. In some places they were more like launching ramps. At least a dozen drivers and riding mechanics lost their lives in the early 1930s when their cars slid high in a turn, hit a more sharply angled lip, and hurtled over the wall.

The fix finally occurred before the 1936 race, when parts of the track were patched in asphalt and all four corners rebuilt. Those steeply inclined lips were redone to conform to the 9-degree, 12-minute angle of the rest of the corner, and the walls adjacent to them slanted slightly inward so they were perpendicular to the banking. Inside retaining walls were torn out, to be replaced with broad oiled-dirt aprons.

George Stewart (aka Leon Duray) and his riding mechanic C. Lyon look jaunty in this photo, but they didn't make the 1932 race.

Hudson is among the carmakers with factory entries in the 1932 race. Here's a passenger car and a race car parked side by side. Hudson's racing prowess was its hallmark for more than 20 years.

Thirty-eight racers take a parade lap behind the Cord pace car in 1930. Rules now require a riding mechanic.

A four-wheel-drive truck pulls several cars through flood waters in 1933.

Drivers Ernie Triplett and Deacon Litz paddle a canoe through the flooded first turn a few days before the 1933 race.

Asphalt is covering brick and a broad apron replaces inside walls through the south chute following the 1935 race. It's the first major track rehab since the mid-'20s.

Other measures were initiated in the interest of safety. Battery-powered green and yellow signal lights were installed around the track. Steel helmets were made mandatory for drivers and riding mechanics. And a driver's test was mandated for all newcomers.

The effect was immediate. After a string of deadly years, nobody was even badly hurt in 1936.

A few other things about the '36 race tickle the fancy of history buffs. Louis Meyer won it, making him the Speedway's first three-time winner.

He was directed when it was over into a new fenced-in and gated grassy plot that had been set aside for post-race folderol. It was known for years thereafter as the "bull pen."

When Wilbur Shaw kills his engine during a pit stop, Kelly Petillo takes the lead in 1935. He holds on to win when a light rain brings out the caution flag.

Among the casualties of the Great Depression is the Speedway's $20,000 lap prize fund in 1932. For years, drivers have received $100 for every lap they lead. Typically subscribed by Indianapolis businesses and individuals, the fund is short by at several thousand dollars when Henry Ford learns about it the day before the race. He writes a $5,000 check.

Whether actual sponsor names or objects of whimsy, verbiage is becoming more prevalent on the race cars of the 1930s. Al Gordon's Cocktail Hour Cigarette Spl. starts 2nd and finishes 30th in 1935.

World renowned aviation pioneer Amelia Earhart visits the Speedway in 1935. She was the honorary referee.

This 1935 photo puts the corner banking in perspective. Note the sagging fence and the weeds amid the brick. A major rehab effort will result in a much safer track in 1936.

Outer walls will be reconfigured and inner walls gone by spring 1936.

He slaked his thirst from a bottle of buttermilk, and the milk-drinking ritual he started is still part of the victory ceremony.

He was the first 500 winner to be presented with the Borg-Warner Trophy, which remains today the most famous symbol of victory in motorsport.

And on top of all that, he was the first winner to be awarded the pace car—or a reasonable facsimile, anyway.

Wilbur Shaw, who would play a starring role in the rescue of the Speedway after World War II, was just another driver in search of his first 500 victory in 1937, when he held off Ralph Hepburn to win by a tick over two seconds. It was the closest Indy finish to date.

Shaw planned his races carefully. He would calculate a speed he thought it would take to win, then drive at that pace with little heed to what others were doing. In 1938, he thought 115 mph would win the race. He ended up averaging 115.580. But Floyd Roberts averaged 117.2, and beat Wilbur by almost three laps.

The 1939 race looked good for Louis Meyer, who was trying for an unprecedented fourth Indy 500 win, until Shaw got by him with 15 laps to go. Meyer gave chase. He shredded a tire on the 198th lap and crashed into a wooden fence on the inside of the track. He was flung from the car, leaving his shoes behind. He said later it was on the walk to the ambulance that he decided it was time to retire.

Although Europe was already in the throes of World War II, Captain Eddie Rickenbacker decided to go ahead with the 1940 race. A crowd favorite was the No. 49 blue and silver Maserati, an Italian car whose drivers, Rene LeBegue and Rene Dreyfus, were on leave from the French army. It finished tenth.

**The second Pagoda is 10 years old and still looking spiffy in 1936.**

For what is believed the first time in motor racing history, the flag signaling the start of the race in 1930 is green instead of red. In a revision of signal protocol that takes some getting used to, red now means "Everybody stop!" Yellow replaces blue as the caution flag and blue now signals the start of the last lap. More changes occur in 1937, when a white flag replaces blue and a black flag tells a driver to make a pit stop immediately.

**For several years in the 1930s, refrigerator manufacturer Norge places several of its products along pit row for use by teams and officials.**

From Turn 1, above, here's a view of the field forming behind the Packard pace car in 1936. From this year forward, the pace car or a replica is awarded to the winner. After a massive rehab of all four corners, that's fresh concrete along the outer wall, but the patchwork of bricks and asphalt still makes for a rough ride. From the bridge over the backstretch, the field begins to close up on the pace car, at far right.

A light rain fell late in the race, which ended under caution with Wilbur Shaw once again ahead. The popular native of nearby Shelbyville, Indiana, thus became the first person to win back-to-back 500s.

A pit scene from 1936, in the photo at top. In the 1930s, this straight truck, above, is the equivalent of a modern-day 18-wheel transporter.

The Borg-Warner Trophy.

The sterling silver Borg-Warner Trophy, originally standing 51 inches tall and weighing 80 pounds, is unveiled February 16, 1936 at the Roosevelt Hotel in New York. It is valued at $10,000.

Those specks concentrated around the inside of the track in this aerial view on race day, 1936, are people and cars.

Eccentric millionaire playboy Joel Thorne, who already has four cars in the race and four more which couldn't qualify, buys Cliff Bergere's Red Lion Special, which is due to start 16th in 1937. He announces he is withdrawing it and putting in its place another car he had tried unsuccessfully to qualify. The Speedway's Eddie Rickenbacker tells him he can't do that. "Keep up the tough talk and I'll buy the whole blasted starting field," Thorne retorts. "Try a stunt like that," says Rickenbacker, "and you'll run your next AAA race when you're ninety-seven." Thorne reconsiders. Bergere gets to start. He ends up fifth, but Thorne receives none of the prize money. It turns out his check bounced.

A wicked fire that destroyed part of one row of garages got race day off to a bad start in 1941. It would get worse for Wilbur Shaw. A faulty wheel had been marked and set aside, but water from the fire hoses obliterated the mark. Somehow, the wheel got on the car, and that's believed to be the one that failed on lap 152, sending Wilbur backward into the wall. He was running far out in front at the time. The crash left him temporarily paralyzed from the waist down. His Indy 500 race driving days were over.

Captain Eddie Rickenbacker wasn't doing that well, either. He had used up another of his nine lives in a plane crash in February. Still confined to a hospital bed, he spoke via telephone to the crowd over the track's public address system.

Winner Louis Meyer in 1936. Close confines, wire enclosure and strict security contribute to the "bull pen" nickname the media applies in the late 1930s to Victory Lane.

1936 winner Louis Meyer shakes hands with the Speedway's Seth Clein during a presentation of the brand-new Borg-Warner Trophy. With them is Fred Lockwood of Borg-Warner.

The infield crowd in 1938.

Chris Economaki, 17, of Ridgewood, NJ, scrapes together $15 and joins two buddies on a week-long trip to the 1938 race. A mysterious stranger gives him a garage pass. His share of the room rent is $1. He buys food and a third of the gasoline, and comes home with $3. He's back in 1950 as a reporter for the *National Speed Sport News.* He hasn't missed a 500 since then. From 1969 through the mid-80s, he is on the ABC telecasting team. The interview room at the Speedway's press center is named after him.

**Floyd Roberts, 1938 winner, is directed into the crowded Victory Lane.**

This scene along 16th Street in the late '30s is taken the day before the race.

Driver Ralph Hepburn in a 1938 photo of the revolutionary rear-engine Miller.

Rickenbacker was in his New York office December 7, 1941, when he heard Pearl Harbor had been attacked. It appears he immediately offered to turn the Speedway over to the war department. When he learned it wasn't wanted, he shut the place down. He instructed Pop Myers to close the downtown Indianapolis office, and he put his brother Al in charge as a sort of caretaker at the track. For the next four years, about the only action around the boarded up hulk at the corner of Georgetown and 16th Street was on the scruffy golf course.

Once in a while, when it rained really hard, neighborhood kids who were brave enough would slip between the rotting boards and head for one of the long, low tunnels under the weed-choked track. There they would swim until the water slowly drained away.

**In the never-ending search for that special view of the race, you do what you gotta do.**

The day after 340,000 British and French military are evacuated from Dunkirk in 1940, French soldiers Rene Dreyfus and Rene LeBegue finish 10th at the 500 co-driving a sister car to Wilbur Shaw's Maserati. Advised not to go home, Dreyfus stays and joins the U.S. army. Le Chanteclair, the New York restaurant he opens after the war, becomes a famous watering hole for racing and auto industry insiders.

**A back stretch scene in 1939 showcases the scaffolding talents of race fans. It's one thing navigating a farm truck into a front-row position and then laying some plank across the stock rack. But check out those even taller scaffolds to the rear.**

Meanwhile, Wilbur Shaw, who was by now too old for military service, had taken an executive position with the Firestone Tire and Rubber Co. in Akron, Ohio. Sometime in late 1944, Firestone obtained a government blessing to begin testing a new synthetic rubber tire.

So it was that Shaw soon found himself clearing weeds and brush off enough of the dilapidated track so he could safely lap the place. He did a chilly 500 miles in an old Miller racer shod with experimental passenger car tires in just over five hours, and fretted every minute about the Speedway's terrible condition.

Counting acreage purchased since 1909, the facility now comprised 433 acres.

A late 1930s view of the iconic Pagoda. It appears the hectic day has taken its toll on a few stalwart fans.

The 1939 nursing corps, at left. If you volunteered to work the race, you got a free ticket and a box lunch. Above is the main gate crew in '39.

Car owner Mike Boyle, the Chicago labor union boss, has an off-site garage in 1939. Ted Horn drives the No. 4 car. The No. 2 car is Wilbur Shaw's. It wins.

"It reminded me of a dilapidated back house on an abandoned farm," he said. He left the track that day vowing not to let it die.

"To me, the track was the world's last great speed shrine, which must be preserved at any cost," he said. "I felt that all I was, or ever hoped to be, I owed to the Indianapolis 500-mile race."

Awhile later, Shaw had an audience with Rickenbacker in New York. "How much money will it take to buy the Speedway?" Shaw asked.

"I'll sell it for exactly what I've put into it," Rickenbacker replied.

With Rickenbacker's blessing, Shaw studied the financial picture and counseled with the Indiana National Bank about how much money could be borrowed on the property.

He prepared a prospectus detailing receipts and expenses at the track going back to 1928 along with an estimate of the cost of getting the place ready to race again.

One of Harry Miller's three rear-engine entries in 1939 is reduced to a skeleton when a gas tank bursts in a crash during practice.

Circulating it to potential buyers, he found a fair amount of interest. There was talk of housing developments and shopping centers, but Shaw also heard from companies wanting to use the track as a private test facility.

He, on the other hand, wanted to save it for the public and for more 500-mile races.

It was an Indianapolis investment banker named Homer Cochran who finally got Shaw and Anton Hulman Jr. together. Hulman was "Tony" to his family and wide circle of friends. The family wholesale grocery business had prospered since his German immigrant grandfather had started it in 1850. Clabber Girl baking powder was (and is) a Hulman property.

In early October 1945, Wilbur drove down from Akron, picked up Homer, and they headed west on the National Road to Terre Haute, Indiana. Waiting for them were Hulman, his top financial man, Joseph R. Cloutier; his personal attorney, Leonard Marshall; Joseph Quinn, head of the Terre Haute Gas Company, and a family friend and real estate broker, Tom Doherty.

Shaw thought the meeting went well. It was nice to hear Tony talk about returning the Speedway to its bygone grandeur, but what Shaw especially liked was the absence of Hulman ties to the auto industry.

**It's a textbook start to the 1940 race. As they cross the starting line in near perfect formation, Mauri Rose is on the outside of the front row, Wilbur Shaw is in the middle and Rex Mays has the pole. Shaw will win the race.**

"He would be free to do whatever was necessary for the good of the Speedway and racing in general," Shaw said.

He felt good about the prospect the track might survive after all. At 11:30 a.m., Wednesday, November 14, 1945, the parties got together in the Indianapolis Athletic Club near downtown.

By 4 p.m., the deal was done.

For somewhere around $750,000, less than $2,000 an acre, the Indianapolis Motor Speedway had become a wholly-owned subsidiary of a wholesale grocery company. Sixty four years later, it still is.

What did Rickenbacker do with the money he got from Hulman? Author David Lewis says Rickenbacker used his share to satisfy a capital gains requirement on some Eastern Airlines stock options he had received before the war.

**The homeward-bound crowd meanders behind Grandstand B in 1940.**

The Payday candy bar people sponsor Billy Devore's car in 1941.

Deacon Litz, George Barringer and Wilbur Shaw examine the charred remains of Barringer's car following a garage fire on the morning of the 1941 race.

Wilbur Shaw.

Among the items lost in a 1941 fire that ravages the garage area race day morning are a pair of scruffy old shoes Wilbur Shaw has worn to race in for so long he considers them a good-luck charm. He is wearing a pair of back-up brogans when he is partially paralyzed in a late-race crash that ends his driving career.

After four years of silence, the start of the 1946 Indy 500 heralds a new era at the Brickyard.

The "Racing Capital of the World" looks like anything but in late 1945.

CHAPTER 9

# TONY'S TEAM WORKS A MIRACLE

Tony Hulman, center, with grounds superintendent Jack Fortner and safety director Joe Quinn, watch workmen clear away weeds and debris in preparation for the 1946 resumption of the Indy 500.

Wilbur Shaw had a description for when the workload mushroomed and workdays stretched interminably. "Duesenberg days," he called them. They were the norm when he worked for the great Augie Duesenberg in the early 1930s.

"We'd report for duty early each morning, take time off for hamburgers and coffee late in the afternoon, and then rush back to the shop to start the night shift. About 2 or 3 a.m., Augie would put his tools aside and say, 'Well, boys, let's knock off and get a good night's sleep. Be back about 7:30.' "

Tony Hulman poses for his first official photo as new Speedway owner in March 1946.

Despite the triumph of sheer will over tremendous adversity, the first Indy 500 of the Hulman era in 1946 is not universally acclaimed. Tony Hulman receives more than 1,000 letters of complaint. One is from a man whose overheated car was stuck in traffic. He said he never saw a single lap. By the time he found water for his car the race was over. So he turned around and went home.

What developed immediately after Tony Hulman bought the Speedway made Wilbur's Duesenberg days seem like a grade school recess.

Nobody remembers ever seeing one, but if there were such a thing as an organization chart, it would have Tony as CEO with Shaw as president and general manager. Pop Myers and the sainted Dolly Dallenbach were still aboard, Pop as vice-president, Dolly as office manager. Jack Fortner agreed to return as grounds superintendent. Don Burge was hired as ticket manager.

Joe Quinn, who had been in on the first meeting between Hulman and Shaw, became safety director.

Al Bloemker, a veteran *Indianapolis Star* sportswriter who had recently opened a PR firm, got called in to deal with the sudden rash of press matters and stayed on for four decades. He would become an institution by himself.

In a move that suggested the Hulman group was a quick study when it came to Speedway operations, the concession rights at the track were almost immediately

**New Speedway owner Tony Hulman, far left, checks out plans for the track in 1946 with his second-in-command, President Wilbur Shaw.**

WFBM does the first live television report from the Indy 500 in 1949.

**Driver Harry McQuinn poses with Speedway President Wilbur Shaw after landing his plane on the track in 1946. Notice the grass growing through the bricks.**

awarded to Louis, Marvin and Charles Jacobs, the famous Sportservice brothers, in Buffalo, NY. Wilbur Shaw used some of the proceeds to finance the resuscitation of the property.

And the place desperately needed it. The garages, damaged in the fire of 1941, had to be rebuilt, along with the old paddock and another grandstand. Six other stands and the Pagoda needed major repairs.

Shaw got hit early on with news that post war materials shortages would threaten the rehab.

New grandstands called for high-grade steel. Contractors told him there wasn't enough in the entire country to do the job.

Then, Harry Tousley stopped by with an elegant solution: Redesign the stands around the kind of steel that *was* available.

**Actress Carole Landis is shown here with Tony Hulman in 1947.**

**Opera star James Melton's powerful rendition in 1947 of "Back Home Again in Indiana" starts another Indy 500 tradition. Bands had played the tune for years during pre-race festivities, but no one had sung the words.**

Less than 45 days later, Harry had the needed material lined up, and Wilbur signaled the Tousley Construction Co. to start work. It was the dead of winter, and the race to May was underway. In the snow and cold, work went on from daylight till dark.

It so happened that a short strike at GM's nearby Allison Transmission plant created a brief but useful manpower pool. Fortner dipped into it. Almost overnight he had an army of men working with saws, scythes and hoes undoing the havoc Mother Nature had visited upon almost a square mile of Speedway property.

Meanwhile, dozens of carpenters dismantled what couldn't be salvaged and fixed up what could. Some of the same neighborhood boys who used to slip through the boards to swim in the tunnels, hunt rabbits in the undergrowth and search for mushrooms amid the rubble got part-time jobs pulling weeds from between the bricks on the track.

Bob Cassaday, who was a Speedway High School junior at the time, found himself crawling over the decrepit grandstands along with two carpenters. "They had these big hatchets. One by one they would tap the boards. If it was rotten, they'd chop it out. My job was to keep them supplied with new boards. So I'd hand one to them, they would put a couple of nails in it, and we'd go on to the next one," he said.

Meanwhile, the Speedway's race against time was making news around the world. Ticket sales surged. By mid-March, even the seats in the as-yet unfinished grandstands were spoken for. Shaw began to worry about crowd control.

The track itself was in pretty good shape on May 1, but the rest of the facility was a mess, so cars were permitted to practice even though opening day was postponed until the 15th.

**Even in 1946 and even if you are millionaire Coca-Cola bottler and Hulman confidant Chapman S. Root, you sign a liability release when you obtain your race credential.**

**Indianapolis Motor Speedway Corporation**

**RELEASE FROM LIABILITY**

Card 0906
Track Pass 0765

Date May 15 1946

Chapman S. Root, in signing this agreement and in consideration of the right to use the track and/or in consideration of the right to compete for the prizes and trophies to be awarded, elects to use said track at his or its own risk and thereby releases and discharges Indianapolis Motor Speedway Corporation, the Contest Board and the American Automobile Association, together with their successors, assigns, officers, agents and employees, from all liability for injuries to person, property or reputation, suffered by him or by his employees as a result of the race or races, or tests or events, or practice or preparation therefor, and whether caused by any condition of the track or grounds or the conduct of any officer, agent, representative or employee of the Indianapolis Motor Speedway Corporation or the American Automobile Association or A. A. A. Contest Board engaged in any matter connected with the preparation for, supervision of, or conduct of said race or races, tests or events, and hereby agrees that the Indianapolis Motor Speedway Corporation shall have the right to take, use and copyright for any purpose whatsoever all motion pictures and still photographs of him by its representatives including the right to make and use reproductions of all or any part thereof and alterations and additions thereto.

Witnesses:

Signed Chapman S. Root
(Sign full name)

Address RR 2 Allendale

Capacity
(State whether driver, mechanic, or entrant, etc.)

**A broken guardrail and broken car are mute evidence of Rudi Caracciola's near-fatal crash during practice in 1946. The famous European racer convalesced for months at Tony Hulman's Terre Haute, Indiana, lodge.**

With a ticket like this and $3, you could get into the Speedway for the 1946 race.

Almost all the entries were pre-war vintage, but two were new. Lou Fageol's Twin Coach Special was a real oddball. It had two engines—one in front of the driver, one behind. The other car was a front-wheel-drive Kurtis body wrapped around a beefed-up old Bud Winfield engine. It was so late arriving that it almost missed qualifying. When it finally did arrive, it became an instant Speedway legend.

Of course, it was the Novi.

Tom Carnegie, who would become another legend, was a rookie PA announcer in 1946. For the next 61 years, his great booming voice would validate the goings-on at the Speedway.

He doesn't remember being on the mic when Ralph Hepburn took to the track for his qualifying run, so spectators would have to wait a while for his signature voice-of-God "It's a neeeww… traAAK… RECORD" pronouncements. But his big baritone voice would have been drowned out anyway by the unearthly shriek from the supercharged 510 horsepower Novi engine.

For sure, Hepburn was on it.

Still way ahead of its time, one of Harry Miller's pre-war rear-engine creations is back for the 1946 Indy 500. Owned by automotive entrepreneur Preston Tucker and driven by George Barringer, the Tucker Torpedo Spl starts 24th, finishes 29th. This is the car that set 33 speed records at the Bonneville Salt Flats in 1940.

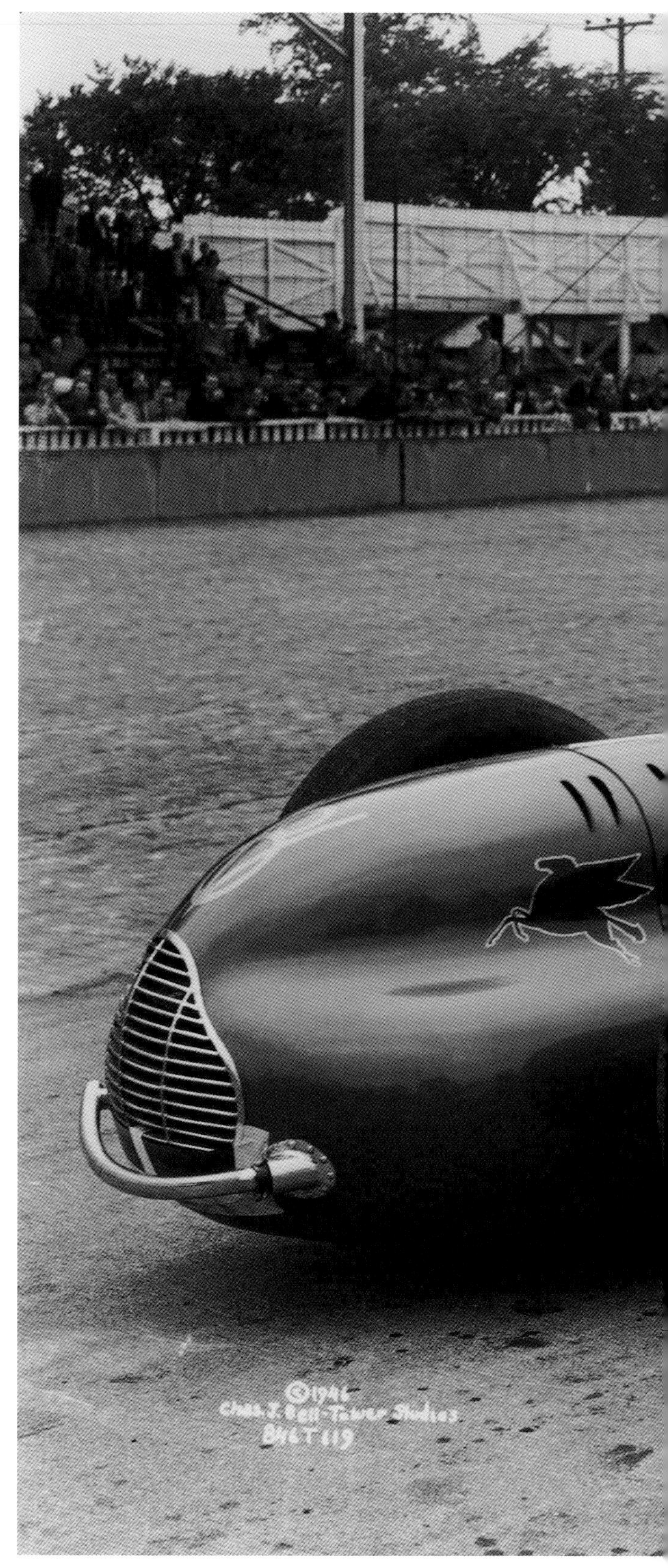

Ralph Hepburn is one of the brave drivers whose attempts to tame the mighty Novi after World War II made them legends. In 1946, he raises the track record to 134.445 mph.

Not since 1939 had the Speedway celebrated a new qualifying mark. Until Hepburn's run, the best anyone could do in '46 was 128.8 miles an hour. Ralph's four-lap average was an astounding 133.9.

After its four-year hiatus, the stage was set for a spectacular reawakening at the Speedway.

On race day in '46, the area around 16th Street and Georgetown Road was total gridlock. The crowd estimate, a figment of Steve Hannagan's vivid imagination in years past, was for once conservative. Bloemker called it at 100,000. Nobody snickered.

Three hours into the race, people who were still trying to get into the Speedway were running headlong into people leaving in droves after Hepburn's Novi engine failed and he stopped on the course. He had started nineteenth and streaked to the lead in just 12 laps, but it was steady George Robson ahead at the end.

**George Robson, born in England, wins the first race of the Tony Hulman era in 1946. He will perish in a crash at the Atlanta Speedway on Labor Day.**

Nobody in the monster horde witnessing the action knew it then, but over the next 20 years the mighty Novi, in all its iterations, would crash spectacularly, cause heartbreak, injury and death, and never take a checkered flag at Indianapolis.

Author Dick Ralstin called it, "A most magnificent flop." But, oh, the banshee sound.

After five months of Duesenberg days, Wilbur Shaw was near collapse. He wasn't alone. Everybody was beyond fatigue. In a moment of pre-race quiet, Wilbur encountered a worn out Jack Fortner at his desk, head buried in his hands, weeping.

George Robson faces the microphones in the 1946 Victory Lane as the Borg-Warner Trophy looms in the background. The reporter in the foreground leaning on the car has an elbow in Wilbur Shaw's chest.

Prior to World War II, the act of gaining entry into the Indianapolis 500 after the field fills by qualifying faster than the slowest car is not called "bumping"; it is "crowding out."

# TIMING & SCORING

About the only thing known about the first timing and scoring system at the Speedway is that it didn't work very well.

But Chester Ricker fixed that in 1913 with a clever system that lasted until 1990. Briefly, a ship's chronometer made in 1876 activated a Stewart-Warner timer which printed lap times on paper tape. Until it was replaced with a photocell in the 1920s, a thin wire strung across the track triggered the printer every time a car crossed it. Simultaneously, someone tapped a button and called out the number. Someone else wrote it down. Auditors hovered, constantly justifying the tapes.

The system was computerized in 1971, but there were still buttons to manually operate as cars passed the starting line. As the system became more sophisticated, the scoring process became more automated.

The era of the transponder arrived in 1990. With radio transmitters attached to every car and with timing loops permanently implanted in the surface of the track, the process was completely automated. Upgraded a couple of times since then, the system can measure to within .0001 of a second. On top of that, a high-speed camera positioned at the start/finish line runs at 10,000 frames per second.

There's a scorer for every car and they move to different chairs as their cars change position during the race.

In Ricker's early systems, scoring was a separate function. Today, it is integrated into the timing process, which is automated to the point where about the only thing a person does during the race is monitor the computers.

Not so in the old days.

It's not clear whether the system was in place for that very first 500, but if it were, and you had volunteered to work, you probably got a box lunch and a big card for your back with a number on it.

If yours happened to be 32, you were Ray Harroun for the day. You'd find chair number 28 in the long front row of the crowded timing box because that's Ray's starting position. Supervisors are walking around behind you. They are connected by phone to the people manning the scoreboards, who will move their numbers based on which chair you're in at a particular moment.

And farther back there's a row of seats for the news reporters. They will eyeball your number to track Harroun's movements over the next six and three-quarter hours.

About every 15 minutes, you and whoever's still in the race will rise and move around to reflect the running order on the track. As Harroun, you would switch to 15th and then to 5th and eventually down to the first chair, which is where you will spend a good part of the afternoon of May 30, 1911.

But to the great surprise of many and the relief of the exhausted Speedway crew, the first 500 of the Hulman watch went off with few serious glitches.

Months earlier, when the Hulman team had huddled with Shaw about saving the Speedway, Tony made an off-the-cuff comment that got carved in stone:

"The Speedway always has been a part of Indiana, as the Derby is part of Kentucky," he said. "The 500-mile race should be continued. I'd like to be sure of sufficient income so we could make a few improvements each year and build the Speedway into something everyone could really be proud of."

It would be a long time before business gurus invented something they called the *Mission Statement* and decreed that every enterprise must have one, but in fact, Tony's words have guided Speedway operations ever since.

Without a lot of long-range planning, year-to-year improvements occurred as a matter of course.

Clarence Cagle, whose tenure as grounds' superintendent extended from the late 1940s to the 1970s, said a priority list was constantly updated but that decisions about what got done would be made year-by-year depending on the budget.

"A lot of times," Clarence said, "Mr. Hulman would just come by and ask what we thought about maybe building this or changing that. And we knew that was our signal to do it.

"A big project we'd start right after the race so we could have it pretty well done by late fall. We never wanted to have to depend on good weather in the spring."

At the top of the list after the '46 race was traffic relief. The zoo outside the track was bad enough, but it was total chaos inside. A plan to virtually double the number of traffic lanes through the tunnels was quickly drawn up, and Harry Tousley's guys were called in again.

**Sam Hanks has band leader Spike Jones as a sponsor in 1946. Standing is Gordon Schroeder, the owner and chief mechanic.**

Over the next few years, a press box sprouted along the top of the paddock grandstand, the parquet seating area behind pit lane, Tower Terrace, was elevated and a row of rooms for accessory companies constructed underneath.

A new field hospital was built along with eighteen more garages and three sections of the big grandstand outside Turn One.

The grandstand that greeted spectators when the track opened in 1909 had been redone three times already. It got another huge facelift in 1951.

With the addition in 1954 of seating in a small gap just to the south, the entire front straightaway and part of Turn One was now one long almost uninterrupted spectator viewing structure. There was nothing like it anywhere in the world.

And race fans unfailingly showed up year after year to fill it to capacity.

Vendors seem to be waiting for the post-race crowd at the main gate in 1947.

Chapter 10

# Shaw Carries the Ball

Front-wheel-drive Blue Crown Spark Plug Specials entered by Lou Moore, center, win the Indy 500 three years in a row (1947-49), with drivers Mauri Rose, left, and Bill Holland, right.

Tony Hulman, the aristocrat, and Wilbur Shaw, the street kid turned racer, were to the Indianapolis Motor Speedway of post-World War II what Carl Fisher and Jim Allison were to its infancy.

Shaw and Fisher were of different eras but they were like peas in a pod. Both right-brainers, they were at once charming and feisty. They were small in stature but they dreamed big. Both grew up in near-poverty. They had little formal schooling. They were fiercely competitive in everything they did. They ran on emotion. And they ran hard.

Al Miller stands in his cockpit and watches the action as his car gets serviced in 1947. For a while in the early days, drivers were required to exit their cars during pit stops.

The most anticipated words in motor sport, "Gentlemen, start your engines," were heard for the first time at the Speedway around 1949 or '50. That's indisputable. What isn't clear is who delivered them. Wilbur Shaw is generally given the credit, but many students of Speedway history think a public address announcer named John Francis "Irish" Horan was the first to utter the famous phrase.

Hulman and Allison, on the other hand, were from patrician stock. They were less impulsive, more thoughtful, more logical left-brain personalities. Hulman was a star athlete at Yale. Allison never finished high school. But they shared an uncanny knack for business.

Fisher and Allison, Hulman and Shaw: Odd couples, true. But oh, did they click.

The Fisher/Allison partnership conceived the Speedway and nursed it through the early years. The Hulman/Shaw team rescued it from the precipice and secured its place at center stage in the world of motor sport.

Two workers and a steamroller, at far right, smooth cinders in the garage area in 1947.

What's remarkable about the Hulman/Shaw era is how well everybody seemed to get along.

The makings were there for significant stress. You had the old pro, Pop Myers, whose tenure extended back to the very beginning. To the racing world he was "Mr. 500."

You had in Wilbur Shaw an intense three-time Indy 500 winner with no experience operating a race track, but a lot of strong opinions and the determination to push them through. As president and general manager, he was the boss.

And then you had the Hulman team from Terre Haute: loyalists like controller Joe Cloutier, safety director Joe Quinn, and Clarence Cagle, the grounds superin-

Indiana University and Purdue University bands join during pre-race ceremonies in 1947 to play the National Anthem. They have not practiced together. One band plays in B flat, the other in A flat. They still get a standing ovation.

**It's 1947, and having just won the 500, a weary Mauri Rose must endure the post-race frolic in Victory Lane, then take a pit walk with his ever-present pipe in one hand and Hollywood actress Carole Landis on his arm.**

An idea Tony Hulman had in 1946 to induct racing greats into an exclusive Speedway Hall of Fame is implemented without Speedway involvement in 1952. It operates independently until 1961, when it becomes the property of the Indianapolis Motor Speedway Foundation.

**Mauri Rose poses with car owner Lou Moore and the Borg-Warner Trophy after becoming a three-time winner in 1948.**

tendent after Fortner's death in 1948. They were not accustomed to reporting to anyone except Tony Hulman.

There must have been some differences of opinion, but if Shaw ever felt beleaguered he never let on. Years later, Cagle would say there was so much to do that nobody had time for intramural warfare.

Shaw quickly became the Speedway's public face. He covered the Midwestern civic and service club circuit like a blanket, hitting big cities and hamlets, too. Many times he would leave behind a banner advertising

**From the very beginning, race time has been party time in Indianapolis. This get-together for track executives and the city's movers and shakers features an accordion player. That's track publicist Al Bloemker facing the camera on the right.**

**Talk about a sea of cars. This is an infield scene in the late '40s. An estimated 25,000 cars are nose-to-nose and bumper-to-bumper. It takes hours to get in, more hours to get out.**

From left: Tony Hulman, Wilbur Shaw and Pop Myers in 1947. Myers was expected to be named president when Hulman bought the track in '45. Shaw got the job instead.

the race with instructions that, come April, it be suspended across the busiest street in town. For awhile in the late 1940s and early 1950s, you could hardly drive through an Indiana county seat in the spring without spotting one of Wilbur's banners.

If his management credentials weren't established during the arduous run-up to the '46 race, they were surely set in 1947, when he broke

Radio broadcaster Sid Collins in 1958.

Sid Collins uses the term, "Stay tuned for the greatest spectacle in racing" for the first time in 1955 to signal subscriber stations on the Indianapolis 500 Radio Network that a commercial break is imminent. But Collins didn't coin the classic phrase. Alice Greene, a copywriter at WIBC in Indianapolis, did.

It's 1948 and Billy DeVore drives one of the most unusual cars ever to appear at the Speedway, Pat Clancy's six-wheeler. The idea is to improve traction by putting more rubber in contact with the track. Fifteen years later, the wide tire revolution accomplishes the same thing.

It's 1949. Duke Nalon, shown at left in his Novi Special, suffers serious burns when his car catches fire in a Lap 24 crash. Bill Holland, below, who will go on to win in '49, drives through the flames.

It's 1949 and that's Larry Bisceglia wearing the railroad hat on the guard stand. For the next 37 years, Larry will arrive at the track weeks before the race and park his truck first in line at the gate.

with some of his race driver friends in a fuss over prize money. The driver/car owner group wanted the purse to be 40 percent of gate receipts. The Speedway wanted nothing to do with any plan to usurp authority over any aspect of its operation. A boycott ensued. The registration deadline came and went with only 35 cars entered. Shaw thought another 15 or 20 were out there.

The holdouts expected Shaw to be an ally. He was far from it. "We'll race without them," he declared. It was reminiscent of Eddie Rickenbacker's 1933 put-down in the Howdy Wilcox incident. As one of the most strident dissidents, Shaw was on the other side that time. He was well aware of the irony.

A *Saturday Evening Post* article detailed the blow-by-blow, which got so heated as race day approached that Hulman stepped in to calm his president down. At Shaw's suggestion, Bill Fox, sports editor of *The Indianapolis News*, became a mediator. He eventually obtained approval from the other participants to let the rump group qualify. Nine cars did so a couple of days before the race, but none finished the 500 higher than sixth.

The '47 race was the inaugural for Lou Moore's legendary Blue Crown Spark Plug Specials. They cost him upwards of $30,000 apiece at a time when $10,000 was high dollar for a very capable car. They were low and light and they ran on straight gasoline instead of some of the more exotic fuel mixtures then available, and they got great mileage.

Like the star-crossed Novi that had debuted the year before, Moore's cars were front-wheel-drive. Unlike the Novi, they would actually win races.

Spectators can reach out and touch Rex Mays' disabled car in 1949.

**There's more to see here than the Borg-Warner Trophy. Notice the barbed wire in the foreground and the scorers atop the grandstand. That's starter Seth Klein in his perch above the starting line.**

Upon the death of Jack Fortner in 1948, Clarence Cagle becomes the Speedway's superintendent of grounds. His race day ritual for the next 30 years includes a careful early-morning inspection of the track. He walks.

**Comedians Jack Benny, in seat, and sidekick Eddie Anderson, AKA Rochester, check out a 1950 car with Speedway president Wilbur Shaw.**

**By the time Lou Welch's Novi entries are received in 1950, all the garages are spoken for. Until space is found on site, he trucks the cars in and out of the Speedway every day.**

Driving for Moore in '47 were Bill Holland and Mauri Rose. Holland was ahead of Rose by almost a full lap with 40 to go and nobody else close. Assuming no calamities, Moore saw a one-two victory just a few minutes away. He thought a word of caution might be in order, so he scribbled "E-Z" on his pit board, and displayed it to both drivers.

Holland slowed, but Rose didn't. The gap began to narrow. With six laps to go, the crowd in a frenzy, and Holland's wife on her way to Victory Lane, Rose made his pass. Not until it was all over did Holland realize he had lost the lead and the race to his alleged teammate. Things were a little tense in the garage afterward.

Driving the same cars, Rose and Holland were one-two again in '48. His back-to-back wins made Rose a three-time Indy 500 champ.

The top deck of the brand-new Turn 1 grandstand seems to float above the action in 1951, as the Chrysler pace car leads the field on a parade lap. The cars to the left on the front row look like toys compared to pole setter Duke Nalon's powerful Novi.

Ladies dress in their finest for an Indy 500 in the 1950s.

Tony Hulman accessorizes his suit with an AAA armband in 1951.

Hollywood actress Loretta Young helps Lee Wallard celebrate his win in 1951.

Holland finally won in '49, after holding off another Rose charge with eight laps to go.

Having parted ways with Moore after the '49 race, Rose would fit a couple more Indy 500s into his full-time occupation as a General Motors engineer. The stories are well told of his lunch-hour trips from GM's nearby Allison Division plant to the track, where he would get in a few laps of practice, then go back to work.

His car has no brakes and he has lost 15 pounds in body weight since morning, but popular Lee Wallard is standing anyway as he coasts down the main straight after winning the 1951 500.

He moved to Detroit in '52 and was put in charge of test and development of a brand-new sports car Chevrolet would introduce in 1953 as the Corvette. Later, he would be Chevrolet's top engineering connection with NASCAR.

The year 1947 is also when the Borg-Warner Corp. began importing lovely movie actresses to give the winner a kiss and help present the trophy. Hollywood had discovered Indy long before, though, as movies with identifiable Speedway themes and scenes were made as early as the 1920s.

Over the years, motion picture studios had recruited members of the racing fraternity as extras and stunt men. Race driver Cliff Bergere is said to have worked in more than 400 movies.

Camera crews and cast members swarmed the track for the 1950 race, when Clark Gable

**T-shirts are $1.50 and goggles are free with a $3 helmet at a Speedway gift stand in 1951.**

and Barbara Stanwyck were filming the final scenes of the hit movie, *To Please a Lady*.

But compliments of Borg-Warner, it was actress Carole Landis gamely planting one on the grimy face of Mauri Rose who really kicked the Speedway's glamour quotient up a notch.

Another tradition got started in '47, when Shaw had a big silver cup of ice water instead of a bottle of milk

**Bill Vukovich leads 150 laps in 1952 driving Howard Keck's Fuel Injection roadster, but the car has steering failure on Lap 192 and he finishes 17th. He wins the next two Indy 500s.**

**The question is whether security is heavy because that's movie star Clark Gable in Sam Hanks' car or because Barbara Stanwyck is standing beside it. They're at the race in 1950 to film part of *To Please a Lady*.**

**Fred Agabashian's low-slung 1952 Cummins Diesel has its own transporter. This is an unusual view of one of Frank Kurtis' first roadsters. If it weren't for the windshield and tailpiece, the tires would be the tallest part of the car.**

Drivers and crew members pose on the track for a 1952 pre-race photo.

Actress Janet Greer and singer Mel Torme mingle with the 1953 crowd.

waiting for Rose in Victory Lane. "Water from Wilbur," they called it. The tradition lasted through 1955. In '56, milk was back and it's been part of the post-race ritual every year since.

Shaw solidified his standing in late '48, when he persuaded the AAA contest board to offer two-time 500 winner Tommy Milton the post of chief steward. Then, he persuaded Milton to accept it. He also brought Karl Kizer, a friend from his earliest racing days, aboard as referee.

Drivers, owners, officials, just about everybody in the Indy fraternity, held both Milton and Kizer in high esteem.

Century Tire Co. was what Kizer called his Indianapolis auto shop. From the 1920s

Mari Hulman, left, (later to be Mari Hulman George and chairman of the Indianapolis Motor Speedway Corp.) poses with friend Bessie Lee Paoli at the 1953 race. Bessie owns the No. 16 Springfield Welding Special, which Art Cross drives to a second-place finish.

Cowboy star Roy Rogers has actress Marie Wilson at his side instead of his horse Trigger at a 1954 drivers' meeting. Notice Marie's white gloves.

Actress Arlene Dahl gives 1952 winner Troy Ruttman a smooch. That's Wilbur Shaw on the left.

through the '50s, it was the go-to place for racers in need of goods and services. He could fix almost anything. You paid him when you could. His generosity was legendary.

It is said he bugged Tony Hulman about the need to preserve old racing machinery so often that Tony offered him a job as the first curator of the Speedway's museum. He took it, but he wouldn't take any more than $1 a year in salary.

Like the rest of the world, the Speedway was a far different place in mid-century than it was just 10 years before. The looming war of 1940 had been fought and won. The post-war cycle of inflation, then recession, then recovery that seemed the inevitable aftermath of major armed conflict had run its course.

In manners, in mood, and in all the ways that money mattered, exuberance reigned.

While Wilbur Shaw was spending millions of Tony Hulman's money refurbishing the Speedway and race fans were buying more tickets year by year, a mostly west-coast cadre of ex-servicemen were happily turning wartime ideas and inventions into a new generation of racing machinery.

Actually, technology was advancing so rapidly that a generation was pretty short-lived. Lou Moore's expensive Blue Crown cars were state-of-the-art in 1947. After 1950, they were no longer.

Ted Halibrand's new magnesium wheels were seen first on Pat Clancy's six-wheel car in 1948.

Speedway publicity chief Al Bloemker decides in 1953 that the Borg-Warner Trophy needs a caretaker. He gives the job to Jack MacKenzie, a husky Butler University basketball player who would remain custodian of the trophy for almost 30 years. The very day Jack is hired, he hauls the trophy home to Butler's Sigma Nu fraternity house. He stashes it in his room. Then, he leaves. The trophy is missing when he returns. He finds it a while later being used by his frat brothers as an enormous beer stein.

**Notice how close racers are to the wall as they set up for Turn 1 in 1953 and how close spectators are to the racers.**

In two years they would be almost universal. Tubular shock absorbers appeared at Indy in 1950. Within two years, everybody had them. Aircraft-style disk brakes came on the scene in 1951.

But of all the go-fast goodies impacting the racing scene, Stu Hilborn's fuel injection system might have been the most significant. Adapted from wartime aircraft designs and first seen on a few Offenhauser-powered midgets in California, the system was good for an instant 10 percent horsepower increase and a 2 mph average speed bump at Indianapolis.

Now, tilt the engine 36 degrees to the right, thus moving the drive shaft far enough to the left that the driver sits alongside it, not over it. Then, design a cigar-shaped body to accommodate a much lower cockpit, and you have the car oil man Howard Keck entered for Bill Vukovich in 1952: The "roadster" era at Indy had begun.

Stands are jammed as drivers in the 1954 race head into the first turn.

**Bill Vukovich.**

The beginning of the Speedway's "roadster era" is generally timed from the moment Bill Vukovich's brand-new Kurtis-built Fuel Injection Special arrived for the 1952 500. With its engine tilted off-center, the driveshaft runs alongside the driver's seat instead of under it. The car is a little wider and a lot lower than the others. Vukovich sets new one- and four-lap records in qualifying. He is leading with just nine laps to go when his steering fails and he taps the wall.

**One of the best seats in the house in 1954 is in the shady second level of the Pagoda.**

An exhausted Bill Vukovich takes a drink of "Water from Wilbur" in 1954, after winning his second race in a row.

Chevrolet is the pace car in 1955, so it's no surprise that Dinah Shore, who signs off her popular weekly TV show with a rendition of "See the USA in your Chevrolet," is the actress on hand to kiss the 500 winner. She's awaiting Bob Sweikert in Victory Lane.

Jim Rathmann asks for a clean set of goggles during a pit stop in the 1955 race. He finished 14th, but five years later he would become a winner.

CHAPTER 11

# IN A CRISIS, TONY ACTS

A lot of his Sumar Special's streamlined bodywork has been removed by the time Hoosier Jimmy Daywalt puts this car in the 1955 field. He finishes 9th.

Eleven cars approach the first turn in heated 1955 track action.

Through the 1950s and early 1960s, the indomitable roadster personified Indy. But to motor racing's movers and shakers, the roadster era was about more than speedy cigar-shaped racecars.

The period saw Tony Hulman's vision realized in a steady stream of improvements to the Speedway, and it saw agonizing adversity trigger actions that validated his standing as a power player on the motor racing scene.

The tragic death of Wilbur Shaw in an October 30, 1954 plane crash resulted in Hulman's more direct involvement in Speedway operations and his reluctant ascendancy to the top tier among racing's ruling elite. In a matter of months, more tragedy would provoke a crisis that threatened to undermine not just his race track, but big-time auto racing everywhere.

In late May 1955, the deaths of world champion Alberto Ascari and Indianapolis 500 champion Bill Vukovich in race track crashes came four days apart. Eleven days after Vuky's death, 81 spectators died during the famous 24-hour LeMans race in France. What followed was a perfect storm of anti-racing sentiment on two continents.

**Low-lying Speedway property remains vulnerable to the kind of flash flooding that nearly fills this tunnel in 1956.**

**Actress Virginia Mayo hams it up after leaving her footprints in cement in a 1956 fun moment.**

**Eventual winner Pat Flaherty, Jim Rathmann and Pat O'Connor lead the field on the parade lap in 1956. Heavy rains flooded this part of the track just a couple of days earlier.**

It may lack the visual appeal of the Pagoda, but in 1957, this new glass and steel control tower is a lot more functional.

Tony Bettenhausen's Belanger Motors car is pulled off the track after an accident on Lap 161 of the 1956 race.

Tony Hulman poses smartly in front of the new control tower in 1957.

It might have been the most trying time in the history of motor sport.

Within weeks, the biggest car companies in America and Europe pulled out of racing or went underground. Lancia dished off its Formula One team to Ferrari. Mercedes would padlock its racing operation at the end of the season. Switzerland, a long-time hill-climb hotbed, made all forms of motor sport illegal.

In the U.S., GM, Ford, Chrysler and other carmakers all signed an American Association of Automobile Manufacturers resolution designed to end their racing programs.

Then, the American Automobile Association, which had been sanctioning races before the Speedway was born, struck the biggest blow. It disbanded its contest board, leaving the Speedway and dozens of other race tracks in limbo. AAA was the only sanctioning body for major league open-wheel competition. It controlled literally every on-track aspect

Tony Hulman with Harvey Firestone, center, prior to the start of the 1957 race. In the photo at far right, movie actress Cyd Charisse draws more attention than the Borg-Warner Trophy she shares the back seat with in the 1957 Mercury pace car.

Pole-sitter Pat O'Connor leads the field during the parade lap of the 1957 race. The ancient tree in the upper right anchors Turn 1 until it is removed in the late '90s to accommodate the Formula One road course.

Jerry Unser's car goes over the wall in this tragic crash in Turn 3 at the start of the 1958 Indy 500. He escapes with a dislocated shoulder.

The aftermath of the Turn 3 accident in 1958 that took the life of popular driver Pat O'Connor.

Starter Bill Vandewater holds the green flag he will use to send the 1959 Indy 500 field on its way.

It's 1958 and Jimmy Bryan is now driving the car Sam Hanks won with in '57. He manages to avoid the horrendous first lap crash that wrecks eight cars and takes the life of popular Pat O'Connor. Again beating everybody through the corners, he puts the car in victory lane for the second year in a row.

Grandstands stretch the length of the front straight in 1959. The only part of the track still brick is this section. Notice a concrete wall now separates the pit area.

Fifty years ago, it is 1959, and one of the largest crowds in Speedway history to date watches the start of the Indy 500. Rodger Ward holds off Johnny Thomson and Jim Rathmann to win by 23 seconds.

The start of the 1960 Indy 500.

A jubilant Rodger Ward kisses his wife, Jo, in this 1959 Victory Lane celebration.

Actress Jayne Mansfield is poised for the pre-race parade in 1961. That's her husband Mickey Hargitay to her right.

Tom Carnegie interviews Tony Hulman during a practice session in 1960.

Photographer J. Parke Randall is watching the start of the race in 1960 when he hears screams behind him. He turns to snap a picture of a 40-foot-tall scaffold with 125 people aboard falling to earth. Two people die; 40 are hurt.

Elaborate scaffoldings were all the rage in the 1950s.

of a race event. As a practical matter, no AAA sanction meant no racing.

Two things were immediately obvious: the void left by the AAA's departure had to be filled quickly, and with Wilbur Shaw gone, Tony Hulman would have to make it happen.

But given the anti-racing climate, what would Hulman do? So soon after Shaw's death, did the mild-mannered wholesale grocer from Terre Haute have it in him to stick with the racing game? Having turned his track from a money pit to a money machine, would he opt now to cash in his chips?

In September 1955, the world had its answer. To the great relief of the racing fraternity, Hulman formed the United States Auto Club and awarded it sanctioning rights to the

Fifty years after the first 500, it is 1961, and nobody's wearing long dresses and gloves anymore. These women are enjoying a pre-race picnic out of the trunk of their car.

Larry Bisceglia is well into his "First in Line" fame as he displays his May decal-covered van/home.

500. Then, he reaffirmed a construction schedule that was the most ambitious of any since the track was new. Except for the bricks on the main straightaway, the racing surface would get fresh asphalt.

A combination office building-museum would go up next to the main gate at 16th and Georgetown Road.

The landmark Pagoda would be replaced by the steel and glass Master Control Tower in 1957 and the pit area would be completely reconfigured with a concrete wall and a grassy apron separating it from the track.

Tony Hulman didn't usually say much, and this time he didn't have to. His actions were loud and clear: the Speedway was here to stay.

There would be other times in the years ahead when the Hulman family stepped in to resolve racing industry issues, but the stakes would never be higher than they were in 1955.

Not that the thousands upon thousands of

**Tony Hulman, who was always "Paw Paw" to the grandkids, is photographed with young Tony George in 1961.**

One day in the early '60s, some visitors are walking on the track. The Speedway gets the idea that it might be nice to offer bus rides. Soon, Volkswagen buses like this one are doing just that. A stop at the starting line allows people to get up close and personal with the famed "Yard of Bricks."

**The sign for the Holiday Inn across 16th Street appears to be beckoning to the passing front row in 1961. The hotel's bar is a favorite racer hangout.**

**Jack Brabham's Cooper-Climax finishes ninth in 1961, and launches the rear-engine revolution.**

pilgrims who made their way to the Speedway annually or the millions who spent race day glued to their radios dwelled much on the business side of the sport. What mattered was the spectacle—and being a part of it.

Radio deserves a lot of the credit. It introduced the 500 to the masses. To millions of lis-

Car 52, the rear-engined John Zink Trackburner, draws a garage crowd in 1962. It doesn't make the race.

Car owner J.C. Agajanian joins Parnelli Jones and the crew in celebrating the shattering of the 150-mph barrier in 1962.

teners, it was not the next best thing to being there. It was better. You could close your eyes and let the imagination run rampant.

There had been live race updates from the track since the 1920s, but the formation in 1952 of the Indianapolis Motor Speedway Radio Network created a phenomenal audience. At its height, 1,200 stations plus armed forces networks in Europe and the Far East carried the race.

Through much of the mid-century, what America did on Memorial Day was to gather on the porch or the picnic grounds and listen to Sid Collins and his announcer corps paint exciting

Englishman Colin Chapman and Dan Gurney in 1963. At Gurney's invitation, Chapman had attended the 1962 race. He is back in '63 with rear-engine Lotus creations for Dan, who finishes seventh, and Jimmy Clark, who is second. The rear-engine experiment is now a revolution.

Two-story Speedway Motel opens in 1963 outside Turn 2. Almost a half century later, it is still the racing fraternity's Grand Central Terminal during May.

It's 1964, and the legendary Smokey Yunick is about to send Bobby Johns on a practice run in what he calls his "capsule car." Johns sits in a sidepod. The car is a curiosity, but a safety clearance is held up for two days while officials study the controversial removable steering wheel. Johns crashes during a last-minute qualifying attempt.

word pictures from Indianapolis. Often they were drowned out by the throaty roar of those Offy-powered roadsters. The beasts seemed inches away.

"Stay tuned for the greatest spectacle in racing" was first used in 1955 to signal individual station producers around the world that a commercial break was coming. But with the three-word intro erased, it became the signature description of the 500.

With their senses assaulted via the radio, people naturally wanted to experience the place for themselves. They made race day the biggest single sporting event in the world. They made pole position qualifying day the second biggest.

For many on the front edge of the baby boom generation, the ill-fated 1955 race is the one from which their memories flow.

As grade-schoolers, they had followed the Indy career of a wiry little California guy named Bill Vukovich. He might have won the '52 race, but a steering assembly failed with nine laps to go.

He went the distance without a relief driver on a blistering hot day in '53 to win his first 500. He did it again in 1954, thus becoming only the third driver to post back-to-back victories.

As 1955 rolled around, indestructible "Vuky" was a household word and a hero to 10 year-olds and geezers alike.

He was comfortably ahead in the early going of the '55 race when he got caught up in a melee near the old wooden pedestrian bridge that

Bobby Johns at the wheel of the "capsule car."

Innovative car builder Smokey Yunick brings his unique side-car racer to Indy in 1964. Veteran Duane Carter gets it up to 150 mph, but Bobby Johns crashes in a qualification warm up run.

Andy Granatelli, resplendent in his famed STP pajamas, checks out car setups during 1964 practice.

Pole-sitter Jimmy Clark leads the way through Turn 1 at start of star-crossed 1964 race.

straddled the backstretch. In a heartbeat, his car was over the wall and Vuky was dead.

It was awhile before a subdued Tom Carnegie made the announcement over the P.A. system and by that time, the thousands of fans at the race along with millions tuned in by radio had likely heard the news.

But the race winner, Vuky's good friend Bob Sweikert, wouldn't know until he saw the headline on a copy of *The Indianapolis News* in Victory Lane.

Vuky's army of hero-worshiping school kids didn't cry alone.

Other heroes have fallen at the Speedway, but losing Vukovich seemed to engender in a generation of young race fans a certain bond with the place. It was Vuky's playground, so it was good.

For nearly a half century, the Speedway has offered to its visitors bus rides around the track. Not too many days go by even now without someone asking where on the ribbon of asphalt did Vukovich's crash occur.

The roadster era at Indy might have meant different things to different people. In the end, however, it was about with the machinery.

Vukovich not only ushered it in, he coined the name. He said the car's high-side cockpit reminded him of the "Track Roadster" class of modified Ford hotrods in the southwest.

The name stuck. Frank Kurtis developed the roadster, and A.J. Watson perfected it.

Kurtis' creations won the 500 five times from

The night before the Beatles play the Indiana State Fair in 1964, they stay at the Speedway Motel. Hundreds of adoring fans stop traffic on 16th Street. Before dawn, Indiana State Trooper Jack Marks whisks Ringo Starr to his farm, where Mrs. Marks is doing the morning milking. Ringo opens the stable door. Mrs. Marks asks him what he wants. "Breakfast," he replies. She fixes him bacon and eggs.

**Ford introduces its brand-new Mustang to a salivating nation in April. In May, it paces the 1964 Indy 500.**

1950 and 1955. He was to the early '50s what Harry Miller had been to the '20s.

The late '50s and early '60s, however, belonged to Watson. A.J. had prepared Kurtis roadsters before, but the one he built for Pat Flaherty in 1956 was taller, longer, narrower, lighter and more aerodynamic than the low-slung "lay-down" cars.

That's 25-year-old Mario Andretti with car owner Al Dean, center, and chief mechanic Clint Brawner in 1965. It's Mario's first outing at Indy. He qualifies 4th, finishes 3rd, and is named Rookie of the Year.

It was so easy on tires that Flaherty could get by with three pit stops at Indy instead of the typical two or three. He set new one- and four-lap qualifying records and won the race going away. Then, for good measure, he put the car in victory lane two weeks later at Milwaukee.

One Watson qualified on the front row in '57. In '58, all three cars on the front row were his. From '59 through '64, Watson creations would win every 500. It helped that he had a different kind of Offenhouser engine. The Watson Offy was a lightweight free-breathing 252-cubic-inch package that was almost as powerful as the 256s everybody else was using, but could run at 800 more rpm. Before long, almost everybody had to have one.

Andy Granatelli was an exception. In 1960 he owned Paxton Products, which made superchargers, and he owned the remains of the star-crossed Lou Welch's Novi program. There were two cars now, all rear drive, all still fitted with heavy old Bud Winfield V8s. Andy's engineers supercharged them to where they were making 640 horsepower. Nothing like them had ever been seen at Indy.

After a couple of years of serious tinkering, Jim Hurtubise, Art Malone and Bobby Unser put all three in the 1963 field. But none made it much beyond halfway. Malone managed to finish eleventh in '64. In '65, Unser started eighth and finished nineteenth. Hurtubise lasted only a lap.

And that was that. Granatelli pulled the plug.

Twenty four years and a million heartaches after Lou Welch set a post-war Indy on its ear with those two shrieking Novis, it was the over.

But for Granatelli, who saw a turbine in his future, it was just the beginning.

Driver Pat Flaherty in an official 1956 portrait.

Jim Hurtubise talks with car owner Andy Granatelli before a qualifying run in 1965.

Three Hall of Fame drivers, Jimmy Clark, A.J. Foyt and Parnelli Jones, are nose-to-tail through a turn in the 1965 Indy 500.

CHAPTER 12

# LIFE AFTER ROADSTERS? AND HOW!

At right: Both of these cars are significant to the rear-engine revolution sweeping Indy in 1965. A.J. Watson built the Wynn's car for Don Branson. That's Jimmy Clark in a Lotus alongside. Little differences in their shape are worth a close look. Clark's victory marks the end of the roadster era.

The Speedway didn't do much to celebrate its 50th birthday in 1959. But in 1961, it made the Golden Anniversary of the first Indy 500 a very big deal.

Grounds superintendent Clarence Cagle would say years later it seemed like the logical thing to do. The race was what mattered, he would grin. But it is safe to say the idea of the track as in institution distinct from the Indy 500 had not yet taken hold.

Constant improvement to the facility, however, was still tops on Tony Hulman's to-do list.

He told publicist Al Bloemker in the late 1950s he expected to see attendance double in the decades ahead as more and more grandstands were added. The crowd estimate for 1959 had been 200,000.

A new double-decker Paddock grandstand across from the starting line would be ready for the Golden Anniversary race in 1961 and the wooden fence along Georgetown Road would come down.

The next year would see new grandstands on the backstretch and Turn 4. The Paddock would get a 600-foot extension, and more stands would go up next to it on the north.

Hulman originally considered a golf clubhouse as part of a new grandstand going up on the backstretch before the 1962 race. Instead, a clubhouse was factored into the Speedway Motel project, which was completed in 1963.

A new grandstand outside Turn 3 came in 1964, along with a complete resurfacing of the back stretch and a tunnel beneath the north chute.

**The 1965 win by Jimmy Clark in a Ford powered Lotus, is the first for a rear-engined car at the Indianapolis 500. No front-engined car has won the race since.**

Laid-back Jimmy Clark, a Scotsman driving Colin Chapman's Ford-powered little green Lotus in 1965, leads all but 10 laps and becomes the first foreign driver since 1916 to win the 500. As Victory Lane rituals unfold, he is approached by 500 Festival Queen Suzanne Devine for the traditional victory kiss. He shakes her hand, instead.

**Car owner Colin Chapman and driver Jimmy Clark, 1965 Indy champs, smile during the morning-after photo shoot.**

**Barbara Eden, star of the *I Dream of Jeannie* TV show, gets up close and personal with driver Jim Hurtubise at the 1966 driver's meeting. That's Al Unser right behind them.**

The golf course was reconfigured in 1965, with 18 holes outside and nine inside, and another grandstand went up in Turn 4.

Another grandstand on the north main straight and the first phase of a three-year plan for the enormous Southwest Vista stands in Turn 1 were 1966 projects.

Fourteen new garages were built in 1967 and the completion of phase 2 of the Southwest Vista. It was finished a year later.

Track areas which had not been resurfaced in '61 or '64 got rehabbed in 1969

A new infield press room backing up to the garage area was opened in 1970.

Phases one and two of the Turn 2 grandstands, along with rotating signs and electric scoreboards on both ends of the track, were done in 1971.

A four-lane tunnel under the south chute, the first race track hospitality suites in the country

At left, official starter Pat Vidan is still perched right out there at trackside in 1966. Within seconds he will wave a red flag to stop the race following a big first-lap pileup. Below, it's a cool race day in the mid-'60s or the throngs in the Turn 1 snake pit would likely be less covered up. Notice the manually operated score board overlooking the scene. That tree in the lower left seems no taller than it did in 1909 photographs.

It's 1967 and here are the Andretti cousins trackside at Indy. From left: Adam, Michael, John and Jeff.

A.J. Foyt is awarded a specially prepared 1967 Camaro convertible pace car after winning his third Indy 500. Citing the absence of optional air conditioning and a power convertible top, he opts not to accept it. Two years later, Camaro is back to pace the race. This time the car awarded to race winner Mario Andretti has both options.

If you look closely at this Victory Lane crowd in 1967, you'll find, along with many of A.J. Foyt's family, friends and team members, 500 Festival Queen Janice Cruse (wearing the tiara) and Jack MacKenzie, the fellow to A.J.'s left. For 15 years, MacKenzie has been the caretaker of the Borg-Warner Trophy.

along Turn 2, and additions to three more grandstands greeted race fans in 1973.

Turn 4 was completely rebuilt for '74. In addition, the pits were enlarged and the pit entrance reconfigured, retaining walls were raised to uniform 32 inches and a section added to the Northwest Vista. For good measure, the official starter got a new stand.

Long before Kevin Costner carved his fictitious field of dreams in that Iowa cornfield, Tony Hulman had discovered that, indeed, if he built it, they would come.

And what the crowds came to see in the '60s and early '70s was a racing show chock full of all manner of characters and machines.

To the unpracticed eye, the racecars of the roadster era at Indy looked a lot alike. A.J. Watson's cars stood out; they were taller. But distinguishing between the so-called lay-down designs was tough. If you knew just a little about them and you appeared sufficiently professorial, you could wow a crowd.

Not so the machinery of the '60s and '70s. This was not nuance. This was an in-your-face revolution you could see, feel and smell and hear. It needed no explaining.

Engines, tires, complete cars: the new stuff would not be denied.

And everything seemed to happen at once.

Paul Newman prepares for a scene during filming of the movie, *Winning*, released in 1969.

There's no mistaking the car or the STP crew in 1967. Andy Granatelli and the boys gather around the controversial turbine-powered "whoosh" mobile. Parnelli Jones is effortlessly in command when a broken bearing with four laps to go puts him out of the race.

Actor Paul Newman gets his first taste of motor racing during filming at the Speedway in 1968 of the movie, *Winning*.

A few of the estimated 100,000 spectators for the 1967 500 Festival parade have great seats in front of the Johnson Chevrolet dealership on North Meridian Street.

John Cooper started it. He brought his little rear-engine Formula One Grand Prix car over from England in late 1960 for a few spins around Indy. Stop watches caught driver Jack Brabham at a tick less than 145 mph, and he was going through the turns at an incredible 141. Nobody had ever done that before.

Car owner Andy Granatelli kisses 1969 winner Mario Andretti in one of Victory Lane's most famous photos.

Bobby Unser waves to the crowd after winning his first 500 in 1968. He will win two more.

Joe Leonard has his No. 60 STP car in first place with nine laps to go in 1968, when the Pratt & Whitney turbine under the bonnet suffers a flame out.

The test was enough for Cooper to come back for the 1961 race. Hampered by excessive tire wear, Brabham finished ninth.

The Indy regulars took note. A year later, Mickey Thompson had Buick-powered rear-engine cars for Dan Gurney and Chuck Daigh. Gurney qualified in the third row.

The Ford Motor Company, which hadn't mounted a factory effort at Indy since the embarrassing Harry Miller fiasco of 1935, commissioned Lotus' Colin Chapman to build three cars, hire drivers and crew, and enter the '63 race.

Ford supplied engines, which were hot-rodded semi-production V8s. Chapman kept one car as a spare and put Gurney and future world champion Jimmy Clark in the other two.

In the early 1970s, it wouldn't take a lot of imagination to see the ancient garages as a row of horse stalls at the fairgrounds. But their days are numbered.

Al Unser, who dominates the 1970 race on his way to the first of four Indy 500 wins, goes inside to pass Carl Williams.

Indiana state troopers are keeping order in 1970 as Al Unser is ushered onto a checkerboard tarp in Victory Lane. It's his first Indy 500 win.

To the great surprise of the occupants, an infield outhouse is turned over in 1966, when a pre-race balloon ascension goes awry. A balloon graphic has graced the wall of a Turn 4 restroom ever since. This is how it looks in 1971.

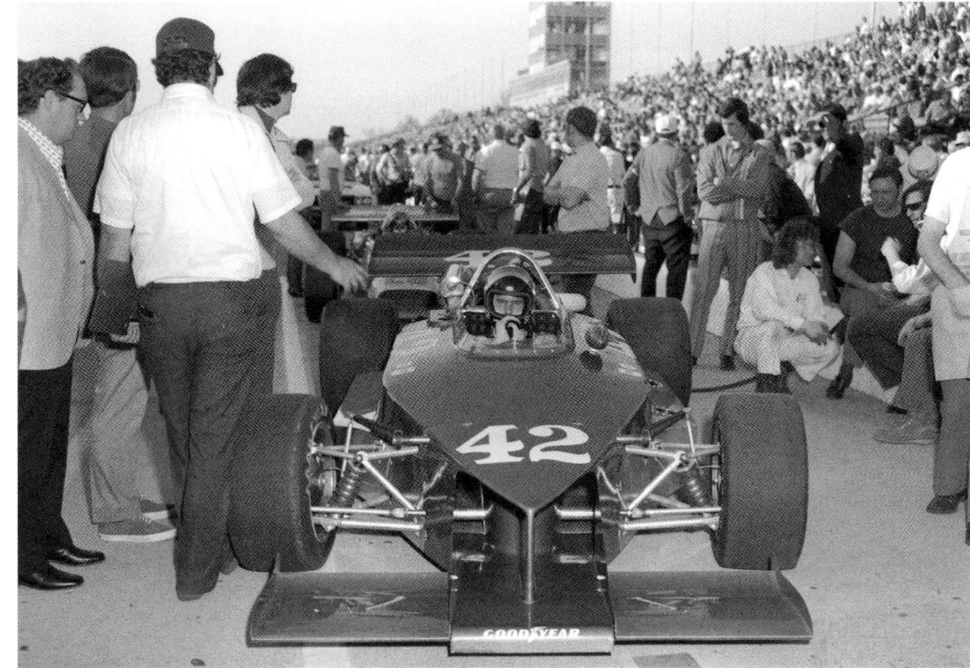


Swede Savage's unusual Manta, aka Antares, racer awaits a practice run in 1972. Savage starts ninth and finishes 32nd, but not in this car.

In his first appearance at the Speedway, Jim Nabors stands on a ladder and belts out "Back Home Again in Indiana" in 1972.

Roger Penske works the pits in 1972. That's ABC announcer Jim McKay waiting in the background.

Clark was in second place and gaining on Parnelli Jones as the race was winding down, when Parnelli's car began leaking oil. Clark slowed to avoid spinning. He finished second.

Ecstatic Ford engineers were ready in '65 with a full-race four-cam V8 engine, which they gave to five teams. Almost everybody else was running four-cylinder Offys.

Clark qualified his Lotus on the pole and won easily.

As an example of what happens when there's a little competition, the Offy didn't die. A turbocharged version came back to run strong in the late '60s, but this round went to Ford.

Famed mechanic George Bignotti, at right, enjoys Al Unser's second victory in 1971.

Bobby Allison, above, is already a NASCAR super star in 1973, but a rookie at Indianapolis. He starts 12th and finishes 32nd.

Mark Donohue is surrounded by a people crunch after bringing car owner Roger Penske his first victory in 1972.

Gordon Johncock celebrates his victory in the 1973 "Greatest Spectacle in Raining." Postponed twice, the race is finally finished on Wednesday. That's car owner Andy Granatelli on the right.

Andy Granatelli is a bear of a man. He sponsors the Gordon Johncock car, which is leading the 500 in 1973 when it is halted by rain. Joe Cloutier is the vice-president of the Speedway. He weighs maybe 150. As Andy begins pushing his car toward Victory Lane, Joe begins pushing back. He tells Andy, "I haven't called the race yet." Eventually, he does, and Johncock has the first of his two 500 wins.

Gordon Johncock.

Next to feel the pressure was Firestone. The company had been supplying tires at Indianapolis since the very first 500, but in ’64, Goodyear arrived. The subsequent tire war found sides pretty evenly split. Putting drivers under contract to use their tires, and keeping them there, was a demanding chore. Firestone shut down its Indy tire operation in 1974.

The fiery crash that took the lives of Dave MacDonald and Eddie Sachs in 1964 brought about the fuel cell, which Firestone had ready for ’65. The cell was filled with a sponge-like plastic. Fitted inside a fuel tank, it controlled slosh during hard acceleration, cornering and braking and greatly decreased the odds of a leak in case of a rupture. USAC also mandated standardized, 400-gallon gravity-feed fuel tanks in the pits.

**The superstructure is going up in 1974 for the Speedway’s Hall of Fame Museum. The rooftop opening will eventually be the location of the museum’s signature skylight.**

**The mid-70s is the height of Indy’s aero era, and car builders are trying different shapes in search of just the right degree of downforce. You don’t have to be a serious student of racing machinery to tell the difference in these three 1974 cars. From the top: Bobby Unser’s No. 48 Olsonite Eagle has a more convex frontal area. The big side pod on Johnny Rutherford’s yellow No. 3 identifies it as a McLaren. The prominent front wing and concave front section on A.J. Foyt’s car 14 distinguishes it as a Coyote.**

The summer of '63 saw Andy Granatelli back in the Indy picture, this time with a four-wheel-drive machine. It wasn't the first. An experimental Ferguson 4wd racer had been tested by Formula One star Stirling Moss in the early '60s.

Andy thought the setup might work in harnessing the prodigious power of the supercharged Novi. Bobby Unser qualified the car in '64, but he was caught up in the MacDonald and Sachs first-lap wreck. It wasn't the last time the Ferguson made news at Indy, however.

In a couple of years, Granatelli would be back with the car most Indy 500 fans alive today will never forget: the turbine-powered "Wooshmobile."

The idea didn't originate with Andy. In the '50s, some Boeing aircraft engineers installed a turbine in a Kurtis race car and tested it at Indianapolis.

In 1962, Dan Gurney tested another Boeing-powered car for Tulsa oil man John Zink. Then, a GE turbine was installed in a Norm Demler chassis, which Bill Cheesbourg tested for USAC. It was thought to be too fast, probably up to 190 mph, on Indy's long straightaways.

But in the fall of '66, Granatelli decided to combine a turbine with the Ferguson 4wd he couldn't get to work in the Novi. He located a Pratt & Witney engine originally designed for helicopters. Rated at 550 hp at 6,330 rpm and weighing only 260 pounds, it seemed ideal for Indy.

British designer Ken Wallis positioned the engine and the cockpit side by side and wrapped a body around it. STP, the oil additive company, sponsored it. Parnelli Jones qualified it on the second row in 1967.

The car was a sensation in the run-up to the race. People speculated that Jones was sand-bagging. It

**Eleven years after his first Indy start, Johnny Rutherford is not to be denied in 1974. Shown here in Car 3 dicing with Al Unser (Car 15) and Roger McCluskey (Car 1), "Lone Star JR" is on his way to the first of three Indy 500 victories.**

Racing icon Mario Andretti smiles for the camera, but 1975 is not that much fun. He qualifies 27th and finishes 28th.

The last two carbureted entries having run in 1963, all 33 cars in the 1964 500 are fuel-injected, but the final day of practice before the 500 will continue to be called "Carburetion" or "Carb" Day.

Hall of Famers A.J. Foyt, Mario Andretti and Cliff Brawner compare notes. Check out the bicycle horn.

didn't take long to find out. Parnelli passed everybody in front of him on the first lap. He was almost a full lap ahead of A.J. Foyt with just two laps to go when a $6 transmission bearing failed.

There was consternation in the racing fraternity. What to do? Should turbines be throttled back or banned entirely? Or be permitted to obsolete everybody's machinery?

Usually, Tony Hulman stayed out of controversies like this, but not long after the '67 race postcards were sent to thousands of ticket holders asking for feedback regarding turbines. There was room for comment and these two very interesting sentences at the top: "I have just viewed the No. 40 STP Oil Treatment turbocar. As a race fan, I believe this car should be allowed to race at the Indy '500' in 1968.'

Of course, turbine power remained legal in '68, but with a 40 percent smaller air inlet.

Granatelli was unhappy, but he commissioned Colin Chapman to build four new turbocars anyway. Joe Leonard put one on the pole with a new track record. Graham Hill was next to him. Art Pollard was a few rows back. Leonard was leading the race with nine laps to go when a fuel pump shaft broke.

For '69, USAC ordered the air inlet restricted even further, and that was the end of the turbine threat at Indy.

But it didn't matter that much by now to Andy Granatelli and his brothers, Joe and Vince. They had other irons in the fire and other cars to race, including by virtue of the STP sponsorship, Colin Chapman's three Lotuses.

Mario Andretti, whose hard luck at Indy was legendary, crashed one in practice. Lotus ended up pulling all three cars, leaving Mario with an old Brawner Hawk to try to make the race. To everybody's surprise, he qualified next to A.J. Foyt on the front row.

After Foyt developed supercharger problems and Lloyd Ruby went out, Andretti cruised to victory lane. Granatelli found him there. A picture of Andy kissing a grimacing Mario made all the papers the next day.

Yes, it's Parnelli Jones' No. 40 turbine car in 1967, but entertainer Johnny Carson is in the driver's seat.

Wings were Indy's next big thing. They managed air flow over and under the car, creating downforce that aided cornering speeds and they accounted in just three years during the early '70s for the greatest increase in qualifying speeds in track history. They jumped an average 20 mph.

The McLaren M16 seemed to work the best under USAC's first wing rule. In 1971, Mark Donohue's Turn 1 speed was 4 mph greater than it was the year before.

Another rule change in '72 seemed to favor Dan Gurney's Eagle. Bobby Unser tooled one through Turn 1 in 1972 at an astounding 183 mph, 20 mph faster than Donohue had gone the year before.

Joe Leonard in his Vel's-Parnelli 1973 car.

14 GOODYEAR
GILMORE
Racing Team
GOODYEAR
GOODYEAR
14
Valvoline
EAGLE
Special
1
Sheraton Thompson
Special
1

# CHAPTER 13

# TONY'S PRIDE AND JOY

Since 1976, more than six million people have visited the Hall of Fame Museum. Here A.J. Foyt's four Indy 500 winners are dramatically displayed in the museum in 1977.

With the completion of the Hall of Fame Museum in 1976, the Speedway gained a crown jewel and a certain cachet. If a place becomes an institution when it counts for more than the events it hosts, this did it.

And Tony Hulman got to see it.

Building projects at the track have always been planned with careful attention to the calendar. What with a few hundred thousand guests on the premises in May, a big job like a grandstand probably couldn't start until after Memorial Day. Because spring weather was always iffy, it needed to be nearly done by December.

Janet Guthrie, far right, enjoys a laugh in 1976 as she makes her debut as an Indy Car driver.

You dare not risk a wet April affecting the availability of a seat someone had a ticket for in May. "Work quick" was the motto.

But when Hulman decided to build the museum, they set aside the calendar. It took two years to complete. Superintendent Clarence Cagle would say of all the projects undertaken during his watch, this was the most gratifying.

Clarence Cagle.

As track superintendent since 1948, Clarence Cagle would say years later he thought he could read Tony's mind. "We were on the same wavelength. Sometimes I knew what he wanted before he said a word."

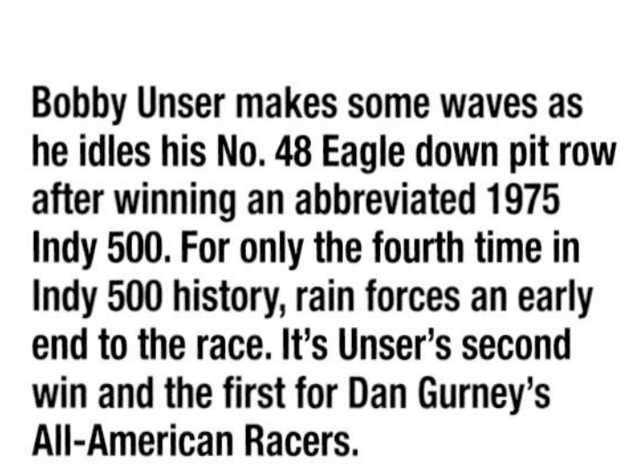

Bobby Unser makes some waves as he idles his No. 48 Eagle down pit row after winning an abbreviated 1975 Indy 500. For only the fourth time in Indy 500 history, rain forces an early end to the race. It's Unser's second win and the first for Dan Gurney's All-American Racers.

It's 1977, and A.J. Foyt has just become the first four-time winner of the Indy 500. He later invites Speedway president Tony Hulman to share his victory lap ride.

Tony Hulman is 76 in 1977. This is his last Indy 500.

Movie/TV actor James Garner is in the pits at IMS in 1977.

Constructed of pre-cast concrete and Wyoming quartz on a foundation many times stronger than necessary to support its floor space, the museum quickly attained an international reputation. It welcomes more than 250,000 visitors a year.

The museum was Hulman's pride and joy. Timed to coincide with the U.S. bicentennial celebration, it opened on April 5, 1976.

Thirty three years later, it houses some administrative offices, two gift shops along with 30,000 square feet of race and street cars and Speedway artifacts. There's also a photo department where the track's three million images are archived, and a library.

Along with the new museum, the late '70s saw the entire race course meticulously repaved, a

A wide-angle view of the storied Turn 1 "Snake Pit" in the late '70s.

300-foot addition to the Paddock Penthouse completed, four new sections attached to the south end of the Tower Terrace and a fourth floor added to the Turn 2 hospitality suites.

The paving project after the '76 race involved leveling every bit of the track to within a quarter of an inch in 10 feet, then applying a superfine, super sticky asphalt surface. To give it time to "cure," Cagle prohibited all except essential traffic for the next 10 months.

Nineteen seventy seven was a thrill-a-minute year at Indy, but bittersweet.

Sid Collins, the legendary radio voice of the 500, and Joe Quinn, whose title was safety director but whose duties made him more of a chief of staff, were both laid to rest.

Mario Andretti, on sabbatical from Formula One, was clocked at over 200 mph in practice, but it would be Tom Sneva, the former school teacher, who posted the first official 200 mph lap in track history during his pole position qualifying run. The huge crowd went berserk.

And Janet Guthrie became the first woman to make the 500 field.

Hulman, who had been uttering the famous words, "Gentlemen, start your engines," every year since 1955, needed some new language. A member of the Hulman family's inner group remembers Tony fretting over what to say.

"It really worried him," she said. "He was so concerned about not offending anybody."

He ended up with "In company with the first woman ever to qualify at Indianapolis, gentlemen, start your engines." Everybody was pleased.

Gordon Johncock, who had won the race in '73 and would win again in '82, was on lap 184 and a straightaway ahead of A.J. Foyt when his engine expired. Foyt inherited his fourth Indy win.

Afterward, he invited Hulman to accompany him in the pace car on a victory swing around the track. It would be the last time a lot of people would see Tony alive. He succumbed in October,

**Veteran Johnny Rutherford, shown here in 1980 after the last of his three Indy 500 victories. He persevered 11 years before he won his first 500.**

**Rick Mears is a promising newcomer in 1978 as he qualifies third fastest for a front-row start.**

**Danny Ongais, the "Flyin' Hawaiian," is severely injured in this 1981 crash, but returns to race six more times.**

Gordon Johncock takes the checkered flag just .16 of a second ahead of Rick Mears in 1982.

just a few days shy of 32 years after he rescued the track from near certain oblivion.

Three months earlier, Clarence Cagle had quietly retired after almost 30 years as the maestro of buildings and grounds, and Charlie Thompson was named to succeed him.

The guard, indeed, was changing. A small plane crash just before opening day at the Speedway in 1978 took the lives of eight USAC officials, leaving many shoes to fill.

On the track, Sneva had the pole for the second year in one of Roger Penske's new PC-6s. Mario Andretti and a rookie from California name Rick Mears were in Penske's other two cars. But Al Unser, now driving for Penske's long-time sports car buddy Jim Hall, came away with the win. It was Hall's first serious foray to Indy. His Chaparral would win again in 1980 with Johnny Rutherford driving. It was Lone Star J.R.'s third victory.

A.J. Foyt and Tony Hulman take a victory lap.

My favorite moment at the Speedway? I guess it would be right after the 1977 race, when A.J. invited my grandfather to ride around the track with him. I was there, and I knew the special feeling my grandfather had for A.J. —Tony George

A fish-eye view of the race day scene in front of the control tower in 1982. There are 500 Festival princesses seated in the first row.

When Johnny Parsons spins in 1983, Mario Andretti (car 3) tries to go around the outside. He doesn't quite make it.

Mini-marathoners pass a trackside water station.

Eight hundred runners pay $5 apiece in 1977 to enter a 13.2-mile footrace from downtown Indianapolis to the starting line at the Speedway a couple of days before the Indy 500. Two-time Olympics medalist Frank Shorter wins. It becomes a 500 Festival event in 1979. The race morphs over the years into America's largest half-marathon. Now staged the first Saturday in May, it sees the field capped at 35,000 runners. The entry fee for 2009: $50.

Rick Mears has just won his second Indy 500 in 1984.

Whether it was all the fresh faces or just a coincidence, some car owners who happened to be together at a Penske party over the holidays decided to challenge USAC's approach to the management of the champ car series. They formed Championship Auto Racing Teams and worked up a rival race schedule.

For many in motor sport, the split that affected open-wheel racing through much of the next three decades can be traced to the fractious spring of 1979. A dispute over entries from CART-affiliated teams in the '79 500 led to several court actions. The teams were permitted in, which was good for Penske. Otherwise, Rick Mears, his new hot shoe, would not have won the race.

Danny Sullivan celebrating his 1985 Indy win.

The famous Dan Gurney is on hand in 1985 with his legendary Eagle chassis.

It's Lap 120 in 1985, and Danny Sullivan is doing a quick 360-degree spin after passing Mario Andretti in Turn 1 for the lead. Somehow, he stays off the wall. Mario goes low to avoid Danny, who pits for fresh tires. They're running one-two again on Lap 140, when Sullivan tries another Turn 1 pass. This time he is successful. He goes on to take the victory. And forevermore, "spin and win" is etched into the fabric of Indy.

# AMID THE MILLIONS OF IMAGES, A FEW MONA LISAS

If you are Ron McQueeney, chief photographer at the Indianapolis Motor Speedway, you make a living in a glamorous warp-speed world. Your main mission, however, is not to create works of art but rather to document in detail the goings-on in and around the Racing Capital of the World. You do that with a team that produces and catalogs a quarter of a million images a year.

But once in a while, there's a Mona Lisa moment.

Asked to pick a few favorites from among the countless photographs he's taken since he took a part-time job at the Speedway in 1972 (he became chief photographer in 1977), McQueeney talks about heart-warming results of careful planning, of perseverance, and of pure luck.

**Wearing white gloves to protect an old photo negative, chief photographer Ron McQueeney checks out one of the three million images in the Speedway's archives.**

**"I thought at first it was too bad there were tire tracks in the snow. But then I realized they actually made the shot so special. They add depth. I shot this from the very top of Grandstand E down in Turn 1. It was November, 1977. Way below zero. I look at this picture today and I don't see a deserted race track frozen in cold. I see serenity. And I shiver."**

"This is late 1983. It didn't take an act of God to get Gordon Johncock's 1982 winning car situated here, but I had to clear it with (track superintendent) Charlie Thompson, who was close to God. He said, 'You want to do what?!' The idea was actually Harvey Duck's. He was an STP PR guy. He heard about our snowstorm and called from Florida. The guys brought the car over from Pat Patrick's race shop on a little trailer behind a pickup. They backed up pit lane to where we had a nice Tower Terrace background. Somebody put the banner on the wall. I don't remember how it happened but we had a helmet. So we put it on someone and got him in the car. You can see the top. To me, that's the little touch that made the shot. From the time Harvey called until we finished was probably four hours. The photo made newspapers around the world."

"If you look carefully, you will see highlights as the light plays across this car. It was a winter in the mid-'80s. The idea was to get beauty shots of the racecars in the museum, but first we needed a studio. The new garages had just been built, so we took over two of them. We put black carpet on the floor and the facing wall and black cloth on the sides. We sealed all the doors. I wanted pitch black. To get the effect I was looking for, I locked the camera shutter open and just popped the strobe lights again and again. It was trial and error. I would run through roll after roll of 2-1/4 film, writing down the settings and how many pops for each exposure. I'd get the processed film back and check the results against my notes. Pretty soon I could predict how many pops I needed depending on the color of the car and the effect I wanted. But there would still be places where I wanted more light, so I'd literally take a hand-held strobe and carefully work around the car to get those details. We practiced all this with the 2-l/4 before we did the final shot with a 4 x 5 camera. It was very time-consuming. The first few cars took us three or four days apiece. In today's digital world, we could do all that in minutes. I think we photographed 20 cars before they needed their garage back."

"It's the middle of the night. This shoot was supposed to have been done at dusk, but we kept experimenting and it got better and better. Working with both florescent and incandescent light in the same shot is always tricky. Notice the windows on one end of the first level of the museum aren't lit up. That's because the door to that area was locked and nobody had a key. You can see streaks of light on the grass and some highlights on the cars. A row of car headlights just out of camera range will do that for you."

"I treasure this shot because it's the last one I took of Tony Hulman. It was October 1977. The event was the annual unveiling of next year's pace car, which would be the '78 Corvette. Nine days later, he died."

"I think this was (marketing director) Bill Donaldson's idea. Emerson Fittipaldi was the first Indy 500 winner to earn more than $1 million. So the morning after the victory banquet in 1989, with armed guards all around, we got him and his car back out on the yard of bricks. And we had a stack of bills worth a million dollars brought over from the vault. Believe it or not, it was not that impressive. So Bill sent back for more money. Soon, a station wagon showed up full of paper bags. And the bags were full of bills. What we had were the gate receipts from the race. I remember I bent down to look into one of the bags and I heard a shotgun cock. I froze. The idea first was to leave the money in the bags, but that would have made a terrible photograph. I said, 'Bill, we've got to get rid of the bags.' He looked around. 'Why not,' he said. So there we were picking up bundles of bills and placing them around the car. It was a memorable moment and a memorable photo. And it got enormous play."

Joe Cloutier, who was Hulman's financial advisor for almost 40 years, had been named the Speedway's interim president after Tony died in 1977. Two years later, the job went to long-time racing industry executive John Cooper, whose considerable communications skills helped keep an uneasy peace between USAC and CART and solid relations with the 500 Festival and the track's numerous business and political constituencies. Cooper served until May 1982.

Finally tired of the bacchanal atmosphere down in Turn 1, where the only seating was on the ground, the Speedway carved out a chunk of space and erected 3,000 bleacher seats before the '81 race. Revelry continued, however.

Over the next few years, the track would build a new Hulman Terrace outside the main straight, double deck grandstand C, erect the huge south vista between Turns 1 and 2, rebuild all 96 garages and add new hospitality and accessory rooms to Gasoline Alley.

Fifteen lighted electronic message boards would spring up around the track in 1987. In '88 the northeast vista would be built.

The racing surface and pit lane were repaved and grandstand A remodeled in '89 and '90. Thirty eight more tower suites would go up north of the master control tower.

A complete redo of the golf course began in 1991 along with an addition to the infield medical center.

Back on the track, 1981 was the year Bobby Unser passed a number of cars as he was coming up to speed after a yellow-light pit stop. Passing during a yellow is a no-no. Unser took the checkered flag, but he was later penalized a lap. Mario Andretti was scored the winner. Unser, who was then driving for Penske, appealed, and 138 days later, USAC arbitrators awarded him the victory.

After all the legal folderol of '81, everybody agreed the nail-biting final moments of the '82 race couldn't have come at a better time. A la the

**Toledo businessman Ron Hemelgarn first fielded a car in the 500 in 1986. He won in 1996 with Buddy Lazier driving.**

**After qualifying fourth, Bobby Rahal wins the Indy 500 victory in 1986. He won after a drag race with Rick Mears and Kevin Cogan on a restart with two laps to go.**

Roger Penske's yellow No. 25 was a show car when it was plucked from a Reading, Penn., hotel lobby and entered for Al Unser in 1987. Narrowly avoiding Josele Garza's spin on the first lap, Unser goes on to win the race.

Famous test pilot Chuck Yeager, hero of Tom Wolfe's ***The Right Stuff***, is selected to drive the Corvette pace car in 1986. Chevrolet offers to compensate him with a street-legal pace car of his own. He asks for two pickups instead. Chevy gives him the trucks and the car.

Ward/Rathmann battle in '60, Mears and Johncock were side by side going into Turn 1 on the final lap.

Mears tucked in behind Johncock as they screamed through Turns 2 and 3. Exiting Turn 4, Mears nosed out. They came across the finish line just .16 of a second apart. It was by far the closest finish in Speedway history.

Rick Mears and Roger Penske make their third Victory Lane visit together in 1988.

For Tom Carnegie up in the public address booth, the finish really was too close to call, so he waited an interminable second or two before informing 300,000 screaming spectators that it was, indeed, Johncock by part of a nose.

After finishing second three times, Tom Sneva won in '83.

Rick Mears was back in victory lane for a second time in '84.

Danny Sullivan survived his famous spin to win in '85.

For the first time ever, ABC carried the Indy 500 live in 1986. And it rained. For hours, network cameras panned the watery scene, as a river of yellow trucks and cars went round and around. The idea was to hasten the drying of the track, but Mother Nature didn't cooperate.

Chevrolet's new Corvette convertible was the pace car in '86 and Gen. Chuck Yeager, the first man to break the sound barrier, drove it. Chevy

Mario starts on the pole in 1987 and dominates the race until his ignition quits with 20 laps to go.

had dubbed every '86 Corvette droptop, of which 7,315 were built, a pace car replica. Only yellow Vettes were assigned to Indy, however. The visibility they got on ABC that day has stayed with them. Eventually 732 yellow Corvette convertibles were built. Among pace car buffs, they're worth more.

Bobby Rahal ended up winning the '86 race, which was completed the following Saturday. He invited his friend and car owner Jim Trueman to join him on his victory lap of the track. Eleven days later, Trueman's long bout with cancer ended.

The pace of change picked up in 1987. Goodyear introduced a radial race tire, and a new engine from a little British company named Ilmor arrived on the scene. The cam covers said it was a Chevrolet because that's where a lot of Ilmor's money came from. It went first into a Penske car because Roger both owned a piece of Ilmor and did the development work.

Ironically, Penske driver Al Unser, a last minute replacement for injured Danny Ongias, won the '87 race driving a Cosworth-powered car that had been in a hotel promotional display just days before.

Ilmor principals Mario Illien and Paul Morgan were both former Cosworth engineers who thought they could build a better engine. Penske got involved when they placed a trans-Atlantic cold call him one late night in the mid-'80s. Their engines would come to dominate Indy car racing and win the next seven 500s.

With Mears, Sullivan and Andretti qualifying 1, 2, 3, it was a Penske front row in 1988. Mears' win under caution made him a three-time Indy champ. For the first time, total prize money topped $5 million, of which Mears received $809,399.

That was a lot of money, but not as much as Emerson Fittipaldi made for winning in 1989. His piece of the pie was more than $1 million, and the Speedway noted the occasion with the famous finish line photograph of Emmo and his car awash in banknotes.

Since the Borg-Warner Trophy seldom leaves the Hall of Fame Museum, the Speedway and BorgWarner begin the tradition in 1988 of awarding Indy 500 winners a "Baby Borg." It's a 14-inch version of the big trophy and it's worth an estimated $25,000. It replaces a plaque each winning driver has received since 1936.

Marlboro
PROVIMI
DOMINO'S PIZZA
30
SHIERSON
BOSCH
TOTAL
EAGLE

CHAPTER 14

# ONE RACE A YEAR? WHO SAYS?

Those 33 orchids on the wreath Arie Luyendyk is wearing in the Winner's Circle are now white. They used to be yellow.

It's 1990 and Arie Luyendyk is refueled and on his way to the fastest 500 victory—185.981 mph—ever. Notice the outside tire changer wasn't required at that time to wear a helmet.

Indianapolis Motor Speedway CEO Tony George.

It was clear soon after Tony George became president of the Indianapolis Motor Speedway in 1990 that whatever was ahead for The Racing Capital of the World, it would not be business as usual.

Almost two decades later, the sacred notion that the Speedway could only host one big race a year is a distant memory. Formula One has come and gone, perhaps temporarily. Its legacy is a multi-million dollar infield road course and other infrastructure refinements.

Veteran road racer Willy T. Ribbs looks worried, but he eventually squeezes into the 1991 field and becomes the first African-American driver to make the race.

The Allstate 400 at the Brickyard NASCAR race is already 15 years old. Motorcycle racing is back for the first time since 1909. And 30 years after a breakaway that split the fabric of open wheel racing in America, the tear is finally fixed.

As Hulman's only grandson, young Mr. George had been training for the job since he was a Terre Haute schoolboy. He was often with his grandfather at race events around the country. He pulled duty during teen-age summers on the grounds crew at the track.

His mother Mari was (and is) board chairman. His grandmother was chairman emeritus. It was his grandmother who gave the annual command to start engines after Hulman died in 1977. Mari has continued the tradition.

Mary Fendrich Hulman gives the command to "Start your engines" in 1983.

Yes, that's a tear on A.J. Foyt's cheek. He's talking to Tom Carnegie moments after his retirement is announced in 1993.

Rick Mears takes a big swig of milk after winning his fourth 500 in 1991.

One of Tony's first missions in the early '90s was to make the Speedway more family friendly. The goal wasn't so much to kill the party atmosphere as it was to give families their own hassle-free space. By the mid-90s, family only viewing mounds were lining the back stretch.

Work began in 1991 on a new championship golf course. A five-acre infield lake materialized in 1992 as part of a total makeover of the Speedway's drainage system.

Bolstering its embankment were huge sections of old track retaining wall that had to be removed anyway to accommodate new structure needed for NASCAR's heavier stock cars.

On the outside of the backstretch, the so-called "polo barns," which once housed Carl Fisher's ponies, went away. They were

Mark Rosentraub, dean of the College of Urban Affairs at Cleveland State University, conducts an economic impact study in 2000 and concludes that three Speedway events, the Indy 500, the Allstate 400 and the U.S. Grand Prix, pump $727 million into the local economy annually.

**Two-time Formula One champion Emerson Fittipaldi adds a second Indy 500 victory in 1993.**

**Higher walls were put in place in 1992 and 1993.**

**A.J. Foyt flashes a big smile in 1994, the first time he started the month of May as a team owner, having retired unexpectedly on Pole Day in 1993 after making 35 consecutive starts.**

**In 1992, Lyn St. James becomes the second woman ever to qualify for the 500. She starts 27th, finishes 11th and is named Rookie of the Year.**

Eight-time Indy driver Stan Fox is airborne in what is left of his car after a horrendous crash at the start of the 1995 race. He survives his injuries, but his Indy 500 racing days are over.

That's not ecstasy written all over the face of Buddy Lazier in 1996: it's agony. Just weeks earlier, he suffered a broken back. Far right: with the hat, the wreath and the milk taken care of, the rest of Arie Luyendyk's victory celebration can go forward in 1997. It's his second win.

A view from above of Eddie Cheever Jr.'s 1998 victory ceremony.

After a long Formula One career, Eddie Cheever Jr. achieves his biggest racing moment with an Indy 500 victory in 1998.

Colombian Juan Pablo Montoya is a runaway winner in 2000.

Helio Castroneves, in the red uniform, and crew climb the fence after his 2002 victory.

among the track's last original buildings. About the only circa 1909 structure left was a weather-worn barn near the railroad viaduct farther east.

Tony had the building completely rehabbed. It is now the beautiful backdrop of the 18th green at the Brickyard Crossing golf course.

He had been talking to Bernie Ecclestone about a Formula One race at the Brickyard since soon after taking over.

But it was the upcoming NASCAR race that pushed his construction people into 24-hour days.

New walls and safety fences, new warm up lanes, a new scoring pylon, all kinds of new communications links everywhere on the property; the list was endless.

On top of it all, the big north vista grandstand was undergoing a rebuild while the splendid brick and glass Administrative Building was taking shape on the corner of 16th Street and Georgetown.

Believe it or not, the really big stuff was still to come. The new 10-story Pagoda and all the suites and garages to the south, along with a 60,000 square foot media center to the north, wouldn't even start until 1999.

Meanwhile, there were still a few races to get the place ready for.

The 1990 race saw defending champion Emerson Fittipaldi on the pole.

Brazilian Gil de Ferran, 2003 winner, seems oblivious to the hubbub around him as he quaffs his hard-earned milk.

Dan Wheldon gets airborne as Scott Dixon drives by in 2003. Both will eventually become Indy 500 champions.

He led the first 92 laps, thereby breaking Frank Lockhart's 63-year-old record. But at the end, it was the Dutchman, Arie Luyendyk, in victory lane.

The '91 race was the 75th 500. Rick Mears earned his sixth pole position start and his fourth Indy 500 win. Four members of the Andretti family, Dad Mario, sons Michael and Jeff, and nephew, John, made the field. That was historic, as was the presence of Willy T. Ribbs. Never before had an African American started an Indy 500.

The new 10-story Pagoda.

Some of the original 1909 bricks are uncovered during a major repaving project in 2004. Monster mechanized equipment makes fast work of the project. Tireless Kevin Forbes, director of engineering and construction, has supervised millions of dollars in Speedway construction projects since the '90s.

This brick and glass edifice opens in 1994 as the IMS headquarters. It's just outside Turn 1 at the corner of 16th Street and Georgetown Road.

# THE ARDUOUS RACE OF THE WREATH

If a floral wreath signified victory in ancient Olympics, the Boston Marathon and the Kentucky Derby, then, by golly, the Indianapolis 500 champion should have one.

So it was that Jim Rathmann found himself wearing a wreath of carnations, compliments of the Borg-Warner Corp., after he won the 1960 race. And every 500 winner since then has found his wreath waiting in Victory Circle.

For the first 30 years, wreaths were prepared by Indy's Cronin Flower Shop. Cymbidium orchids soon became the flower of choice (it's been said someone objected to the cloying aroma of the carnations).

Bill Cronin would make the wreath and deliver it to the track the day before the race. His destination was a room where the pace cars were kept and where his sister Pat held forth. She watched over the wreath, which was wrapped in waxed florist paper and safely tucked atop a refrigerator.

Nowadays, the wreath is displayed on an easel in the Borg-Warner suite until about Lap 175, when it is moved to the victory platform.

In the first moments after the winner gets there, the wreath bearer does his thing. He slips the winner's arm through the center and lifts the wreath over his head. It is supposed to come to rest on the opposite shoulder. In a matter of seconds the deed is done. The hoopla can now begin.

When Bill Cronin died, Dan and Joyce Purifoy's Fairfield Florists took on the wreath project. Soon, a young employee named Julie Harman got involved.

For the last 18 years, through job changes, free-lancing and now as the owner of Buck Creek Flowers in Yorktown, Indiana, Julie has remained the wreath lady.

She gets her ivory colored orchids with burgundy centers from growers Tom and Connie Neilson near Waldport, Ore. They usually send a case of 40 or more, timing it to arrive four or five days before the race.

It takes Julie about six hours to create the wreath out of batches of greenery, tiny checkered flags, some very special red, white and blue ribbon, the hand-crafted Borg-Warner woodcut, and the finest 33 orchids in the Neilson shipment. When it's all done it weighs about 20 pounds.

Saturday morning finds her delivering her masterpiece to the BorgWarner suite at the Speedway.

**Scott Dixon wears his giant victory wreath of flowers.**

**Poised to start a victory lap in 1961, A.J. Foyt wears a wreath of yellow orchids along with a Hawaiian lei; wife Lucy holds a bouquet of roses. That's Tony Hulman in the front seat of the pace car.**

Buddy Rice wins the rain-shortened 2004 race. His victory celebration is moved to the lower level corner of the Pagoda.

Lyn St. James became the second woman ever to make the race in 1992. Her 11th place finish earned her Rookie of the Year honors. Al Unser Jr. held off Scott Goodyear to win it by just .043 seconds–about half a car length.

All-round nice guy Rick Mears, one of Indy's true greats, retired in December 1992, but the Penske juggernaut was unfazed. Emerson Fittipaldi won his second 500.

The year of the vestigial pushrod was 1994. USAC rules permitted pushrod engines to have more displacement. Roger Penske made one act like an overhead cam engine, and Al Unser Jr. won his second Indy 500.

Firestone was back supplying tires at Indy in 1995 after a 21-year absence. Jacque Villeneuve beat

A.J. Foyt IV receives some Speedway driving tips from his illustrious grandfather, A.J. Foyt Jr. in 2004.

Sam Hornish's mangled Team Penske car is on the hook after a Lap 146 crash takes him out of the 2005 Indy 500. The car is designed to collapse on impact, thus absorbing force that might otherwise be transferred to the driver.

Racing four-wide down the front straight at Indianapolis is a goose-bump sight in 2005. That's eventual winner Dan Wheldon in Car 26. Runner-up Vitor Meira is driving Car 17. Felipe Giaffone is in Car 48. Tomas Scheckter is in Car 4.

Indy 500 winner Dan Wheldon is sufficiently overwrought that he opts to do a "donut" on the front stretch before entering Victory Lane in 2005, thus giving him time to regain his composure. Los Angeles artist Ingrid Calame is shown the mark several months later. She executes a tracing on Mylar and transfers it to a full-size enamel and latex painting. The work becomes the centerpiece of the 20 x 72-foot artwork "Traces of the Indianapolis Motor Speedway," which is unveiled at the Indianapolis Museum of Art in November 2007.

Car owners Chip Ganassi, left, and Bobby Rahal, compare notes. Both are Indy 500 veterans. Rahal won in 1986.

Christian Fittipaldi to the finish line by 2.4 seconds.

The debut of the Indy Racing League at Indy was 1996. Arie Luyendyk's first qualifying times were disallowed because his car was under weight. He came back to post a single lap record time of 237.498 mph. For the last time in his long career at the mike, Tom Carnegie delivered his signature line: "It's a neew traaaak recooord." Buddy Lazier won the race.

Luyendyk won the '97 race by a half-second over hard-luck teammate Scott Goodyear. Owner/driver Eddie Cheever was the '98 victor.

A.J. Foyt picked up his first Indy win as a car owner in '99. Kenny Brack was his driver.

Joining Lyn St. James in the 2000 Indy lineup was 19-year-old Sarah Fisher. Their cars got together on lap 67. Neither could continue. Juan Montoya won it.

After a six-year absence, Roger Penske was

TV talk show host David Letterman, an Indianapolis native, is co-owner of Rahal Letterman Racing.

Danica Patrick powers away from a pit stop in 2005. On Lap 56 she becomes the first women to lead an Indy 500. Her fourth-place finish earns $378,855 for Rahal Letterman Racing and rookie-of-the-year honors for Danica.

**Classic Penske strategy has Sam Hornish Jr. in the right place at the right time for his 2006 Indy 500 win.**

back in 2001, along with fellow CART team owner Chip Ganassi. Rookie Helio Castroneves and Penske teammate Gil de Ferran were one-two at the end.

De Ferran won in 2003 as five more CART-based teams were Indy entries.

With tornadoes close by and Buddy Rice in the lead, the 2004 race was called on lap 180. TV talk show host David Letterman, an Indianapolis native, became an Indy-winning car owner.

**Brian Barnhart, President of Competition and Operations Division, IRL.**

**The 2008 pit action is fast and furious.**

A close look at the tiny grooves in the Yard of Bricks reveals the corduroy effect created by diamond-grinding in 2006. The entire track is like this.

Twenty-three-year-old Danica Patrick made her debut in 2005. She started fourth, but it was Dan Wheldon in victory circle at the end.

The '06 race was one to savor. Rookie Marco Andretti, driving for a team partly owned by his dad, Michael, and Sam Hornish Jr. of Team Penske, were side-by-side and nose-to-tail on the white flag lap. Hornish took the win by .0635 second.

Teammates Tony Kanaan and Danica Patrick in a pre-race discussion.

Carl Haas (with cigar, of course) and Academy Award-winning actor Paul Newman have been car-owner partners since 1983. An ailing Newman returned to the Speedway in 2008 for the first time in several years.

In 2007, Milka Duno of Venezuela becomes the fifth woman to start in the Indy 500.

Car owner/driver Sarah Fisher is ecstatic after she qualifies for her seventh Indy 500 in 2008.

Driving for Andretti Green Racing, Dario Franchitti was ahead on lap 166 when the 2007 race was halted by rain.

Starting from the pole, Scott Dixon won in 2008 by less than two seconds over Vitor Meira. It was the third Indy win for the team owner Chip Ganassi.

Marco Andretti carries the Indiana Jones motif on his head and on his car, below, at the 2008 Indy 500.

Michael Andretti.

# Pre-Race Ritual Scripted to the Second

Of all the folderol in motor sport, none tugs at the heartstrings quite like the 20-plus minutes preceding the start of the Indianapolis 500. The ritual has been altered little from when Indy's most senior ticket holders were just kids. It's been memorized, emulated, and, yes, mocked. But to millions, it is a religious experience.

The carefully choreographed 2008 Race Day countdown actually begins when the gates open at 6 a.m. It is precise to the second. Julianne Hough, the dance partner of Helio Castroneves when he won *Dancing with the Stars,* must sing the National Anthem in exactly a minute and 24 seconds. Jim Nabors has a minute, 20 seconds to croon "Back Home Again in Indiana."

The Speedway's front stretch is awash in red, white and blue during 2008 pre-race ceremonies.

On cue, balloons pour into the sky.

Old Glory is unfurled in 2008 on pristine Turn 1, known in earlier times as the Snake Pit.

There's exactly a minute from when Mari Hulman George tells the drivers to start their engines until the parade lap begins.

In 2008, it was 20 minutes and 40 seconds from the time Florence Henderson began singing "God Bless America" until honorary starter Kristi Yamaguchi waved a green flag to start the race.

From an 18-page script Speedway President Joie Chitwood pulled off his printer at 5 a.m. and carried with him all day, here's exactly how those minutes played out:

12:51 . . . . . . . . . . . . . . "God Bless America" – Florence Henderson, Victory Podium (1:30)
12:53. . . . . . . . . . . . . . . . . . . . . . . . . . . . . . . .Color Guard in position – Victory Circle lift
12:54:30 . . . . . . . . . . . . . . . . . . . . . . . . . . . . . Intro National Anthem (Julianne Hough)
12:54:45 . . . . . . . . . . . . . . . . . . . . . . . . . . . . . . . . National Anthem – Victory Podium
. . . . . . . . . . . . . . . . . . . . . . . . . . Flag in Turn 1 begins unfurling 5 seconds into anthem
12:56:09 . . . . . . . . . . . . . . . . . . . . . . . . . . . . . . .Conclude National Anthem – Flyover
. . . . . . . . . . . . . . . . . . . . . . . . . . . . . . American flag secured and removed from Turn 1
12:56:20 . . . . . . . . . . . . . . . . . . . . . . . . . . . . . . . Announcement – Drivers to your cars
12:57:45 . . . . . . . . . . . . . . . . . . . . . . . . . . . . . . . . . . . . . . . . . . . . .Intro invocation
12:58. . . . . . . . . . . . . . . . . . . Invocation – Archbishop Daniel Buechlein, Victory Podium
12:59:30 . . . . . . . . . . . . . . . . . . . . . . . . . . . . . . . . . . . . . . . . . . .Invocation concludes
1:00:15 . . . . . . . . . . . . . . . . . . . . . . . . . . . . . . . . . . . . . . . . . . . . . . . . . . . Intro Taps
1:00:45 . . . . . . . . . . . . . . . . . . . . . . . . . . . "Taps" – Sgt. Byron Bartosh – Victory Podium
1:02:00 . . . . . . . . . . . . . . . . . . . . . . . . . . . . . . . . . . . . . . . . . . . . . . . Intro Jim Nabors
1:02:20 . . . . . . . . . . . . . . . . . . . . . . . . . . "Back Home Again in Indiana" Victory Podium
. . . . . . . . . . . . . . . . . . . . . . . . . . . . . . . . . . . . . . . . . . . . . . . Cue balloon spectacle
1:03:30 . . . . . . . . . . . . . . . . . . . . . . . . . . . . . . . . . . . . . . . . . . . . Intro – Command
1:03:40 . . . . . . . . . . . "Ladies and Gentlemen, Start Your Engines" – Mari Hulman George
. . . . . . . . . . . . . . . . . . . . . . . . . . . . . . . . . . . . . . . . . . . . . . . . . . . . Victory Podium
1:04:40 . . . . . . . . . . . . . . . . . . . . . . . . . . . . . . . . . . . . . . . . . . . . Parade lap begins
1:09:40 . . . . . . . . . . . . . . . . . . . . . . . . . . . . . . . . . . . . . . . . . . . . . . Pace lap begins
1:11:40 . . . . . . . . . . . . . . . . . . . . . . . . . . . . . . . . . . . . . Green flag – Kristy Yamaguchi

Jim Nabors sings "Back Home Again in Indiana" as if he's a born-and-bred Hoosier.

On Mari Hulman George's command, engines roar. The only child of Tony and Mary Hulman, Mari has been Chairman of the Board of the Indianapolis Motor Speedway since 1988. Just as her father and mother did before her, she's poised to deliver the most awaited words in motor sport: "Ladies and gentlemen, start your engines."

Almost indistinguishable in the colorful scene, a line of Corvette pace car replicas eases alongside the NASCAR cars just before the '94 start.

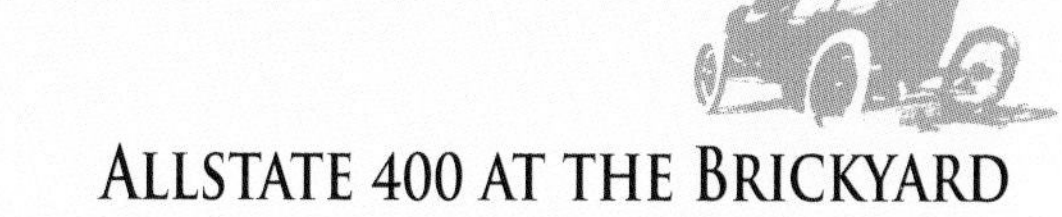



Caught in a pensive moment, a young Jeff Gordon is suited up for the inaugural Allstate 400 at the Brickyard NASCAR race in 1994. Before the day is over, the one-time resident of nearby Pittsboro, Indiana will earn the first of four Brickyard titles.

# NASCAR's 15 Years at Indy

It all started in 1992 with a few NASCAR stock cars descending upon Indianapolis for a tire test. Two years later, August 6, 1994, a quarter of a million zealous NASCAR fans watched Jeff Gordon win the first Allstate 400 at the Brickyard. Here's a year-by-year review:

A quarter-century after his father first approached Tony Hulman about running stock cars at Indianapolis, Bill France Jr., above, has to be savoring this moment alone in the Speedway garage area in 1994.

The legendary Clarence Cagle, Indy's track superintendent for 30 years, attends the first Allstate 400 at the Brickyard in 1994.

Dale Earnhardt Jr. at the Speedway in 2001.

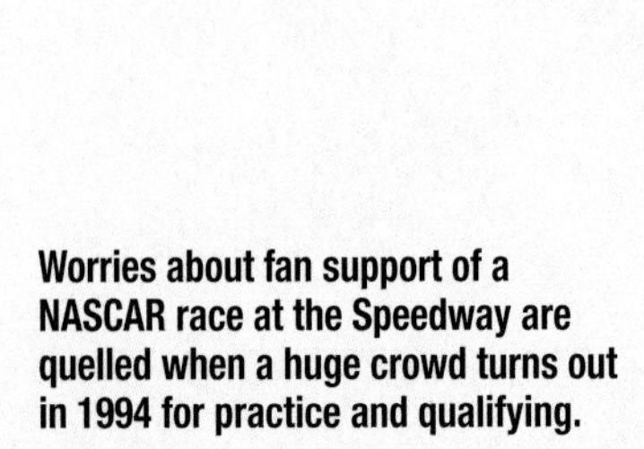

Worries about fan support of a NASCAR race at the Speedway are quelled when a huge crowd turns out in 1994 for practice and qualifying.

## 1994

Rick Mast is on the pole. Jeff Gordon, who had just turned 23, beats Brett Bodine to the checkered flag by .53 of a second to collect $613,000 of a NASCAR record $3.2 million purse. Average race speed: 131.932 mph. “Without tears coming up, I tell you, this is the greatest thing in the world,” Gordon said. “It’s far past our expectations.” Gordon and his girlfriend at the time celebrate with a pizza delivered to their hotel room.

## 1995

After a four-hour rain delay and a fast race slowed by only one caution, it’s Dale Earnhardt in victory lane. Rusty Wallace, whose big lead is wiped out when he is caught in a pit lane collision between Joe Nemechek and Rich Bickle, is just .37 second behind Earnhardt at the end.

**A smiling A.J. Foyt makes the field for the ’94 Allstate 400 at the Brickyard.**

**Jeff Gordon’s place in Speedway history is assured when he wins Indy’s first Allstate 400 at the Brickyard NASCAR race. The Chevy guys with him here are racing chief Herb Fishel, left, and General Manager Jim Perkins.**

## 1996

Earnhardt, who suffered a broken collarbone and cracked sternum the week before at Talledaga, manages six laps before turning his car over to Mike Skinner. Dale Jarrett and teammate Ernie Irvan dual to the finish with Jarrett ahead when Robert Pressley crashes. The race ends under caution.

**Ricky Rudd.** *U.S. Air Force*

## 1997

Ernie Irvan is on the pole. He, Jarrett and Gordon dominate the race. But when almost everybody pits on Lap 114, Ricky Rudd doesn't. Gambling that he has enough fuel to go all he way, he is helped by a late race caution. Bobby Labonte comes within .138 second of catching him at the finish line. Rudd runs out of gas moments later.

## 1998

Jarrett is in command when a pit stop miscue leaves him out of fuel on the back stretch. Suddenly, he is four laps down. Gordon takes the lead from Earnhardt on Lap 127 and stays there to the end. The victory earns him a $1 million bonus from the series sponsor. He's the Brickyard's first two-time winner.

## 1999

Gordon is on the pole, but it's Jarrett in victory lane. As if to make up for the heartbreak of the year before, he leads a total of 117 laps. Bobby Labonte is three seconds back at the end, in second. Jarrett becomes the Brickyard's second two-time winner.

**A.J. Foyt chats with Mary Fendrich Hulman before she tells the Brickyard drivers in 1996: "Start your engines."**

## 2000

It's finally Bobby Labonte's turn. Rusty Wallace dominates early, but Labonte gets around him on lap 147. His margin of victory is over four seconds, the largest in event history. In his last Indy appearance as a driver, Darrell Waltrip qualifies on the outside front row.

## 2001

Starting 27th, Gordon is not a contender until lap 132. Crew chief Robbie Loomis decides on a two-tire pit stop instead of four, and Gordon suddenly finds himself running second to Sterling Marlin. He takes the lead four laps later, and goes on to win by about a second. He's now a three-time Brickyard 400 champ.

## 2002

It's a blistering hot day in Indy. Bill Elliott starts from the front row, leads 93 laps and wins by 1.269 seconds over Rusty Wallace. It's Wallace's third second-place finish.

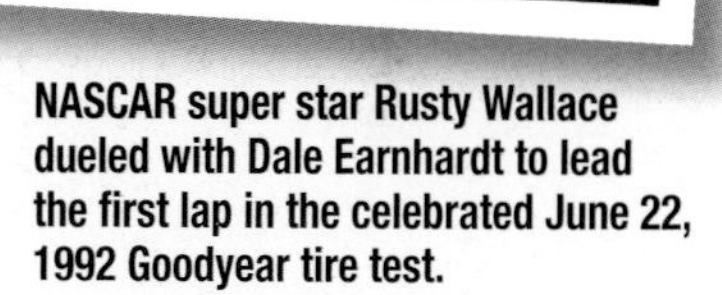

NASCAR super star Rusty Wallace dueled with Dale Earnhardt to lead the first lap in the celebrated June 22, 1992 Goodyear tire test.

Robby Gordon is one of only three drivers who have managed to make both the Indy 500 and the Charlotte 600 NASCAR races on the same day. The other two: John Andretti and Tony Stewart.

Although a few NASCAR drivers kissed the bricks after a 1993 practice session, Dale Jarrett, right, and his crew chief Todd Parrott stir up a commotion and launch a tradition when they do it following his 1996 victory.

Smiling Bill Elliott, "Awesome Bill from Dawsonville," wins the 2002 Allstate 400 at the Brickyard.

Driver Kevin Harvick gets his 2003 Allstate 400 at the Brickyard winner's ring.

A big backstretch crash in the 2003 Allstate 400 at the Brickyard ends the day for Joe Nemechek.

Crewmen hustle to get Dale Earnhardt Jr. back in the fray in 2003.

## 2003

Tony Stewart is running strong when his late race pit stop opens the door for Kevin Harvick. The final 16 laps are nail-biters. Harvick and teammate Robby Gordon both get around Jamie McMurray on a restart. It's Harvick at the end.

## 2004

Jeff Gordon leads four times for 148 laps, including the last 35, to make his fourth Brickyard 400 victory look easy. Bypassing victory lane, he brings his car to a stop at the Yard of Bricks, where a celebration breaks out. Dale Jarrett is second.

The King, Richard Petty, at the Allstate 400 at the Brickyard in 2004.

The Home Depot team celebrates the 2005 Allstate 400 at the Brickyard win along with an exuberant Tony Stewart.

Allstate 400 at the Brickyard cars enter the track through this narrow chute.

Even before the famous Goodyear tire test in June 1992, that laid the foundation for NASCAR's Brickyard race, some IROC cars were on the track in March. An IROC race was a regular feature of the Brickyard weekend from 1998 through 2003.

My favorite moment at the Speedway? Obviously 2005, when I won my first Brickyard 400. But I still get goose bumps every time I'm there. It can be a day when nothing's going on. There's a lot of ghosts around that place that are still working on Offys or old race cars and there's still drivers running around in leather helmets and goggles. When there's nothing going on is when, to me, there's the most going on.
—Tony Stewart

## 2005

This time, Tony Stewart is not to be denied. The Columbus, Indiana native with an obsession about winning at Indy that goes back to his grade-school kart racing days has been so close so many times. This one almost gets away when Kasey Kahne passes him with 27 laps to go. On worn-out tires with 11 laps left, he retakes the lead. And that's it.

A bump on a restart puts Dale Earnhardt, Jr. in the wall and out of the 2005 Allstate 400 at the Brickyard.

Kasey Kahne's jackman turns the corner in 2005.

With walls of humanity rising steeply on both sides, the front straight at Indy is like a canyon. Waving the green flag to start the 2005 Allstate 400 at the Brickyard is TV star Dennis Haysbert of "24" and "The Unit" fame.

## 2006

It's a dog-fight during the last 30 laps, as Jimmie Johnson, Kevin Harvick, Jeff Burton and Kasey Kahne chase each other. Kahne gets loose on the white flag lap and goes nose-first into the SAFER Barrier. That brings out the yellow, freezing the field, and Johnson cruises home.

Tony Stewart starts climbing the fence at the finish line after winning the 2005 Allstate 400 at the Brickyard.

Tony Stewart, who's fondest dream was to win the Indianapolis 500, instead captures two wins at the Allstate 400 at the Brickyard. He is saluted in 2006 with a special display in the Hall of Fame Museum.

Tony Stewart's winner's ring.

Mark Martin: A NASCAR elder statesman.

## 2007

There are six crashes in the first 60 laps. Amid the carnage, Tony Stewart and Dale Earnhardt Jr. dominate. Kevin Harvick slips past Stewart on a restart with 20 laps to go. Stewart tries a pass with 12 to go. He fails. But two laps later, he barrels into the lead for good. It's his second Allstate 400 at the Brickyard win.

Tony Stewart has immense passion for competing at IMS.

NASCAR crash repair; it isn't pretty but it's still in the race.

NASCAR driver Paul Menard obliges autograph seekers in 2007.

Sharp turns and very little margin for error make the Speedway a most challenging circuit. It's tailor-made for incidents like this 2007 Allstate 400 at the Brickyard crash.

## 2008

In a caution-filled race marred by tire wear issues, Jimmie Johnson's crew chief Chad Knaus opts to change only two with eight laps to go. That puts Johnson in front on a restart. He holds off Carl Edwards to win his second Allstate 400 at the Brickyard in three years. It's car owner Rick Hendrick's sixth Indy win.

**Car owner Rick Hendrick accepts the 2008 winner's trophy from Speedway President and COO Joie Chitwood. Hendrick's teams have won six Allstate 400s at the Brickyard.**

**Hours before an Allstate 400 at the Brickyard start.**

Jimmie Johnson is kissing bricks after his 2008 Allstate 400 at the Brickyard win.

Smokey burnouts are commonplace after a Sprint Cup win.

Definition of sensory overload: The start of an Allstate 400 at the Brickyard.

Indianapolis Motor Speedway CEO Tony George and MotoGP rider Nicky Hayden, resplendent in 1909 racing livery, pose at the Yard of Bricks.

With its massive grandstands deserted on a damp morning in July 2008, the Speedway awaits the start of a shake-down session for the Red Bull Rookies Cup riders.

# RED BULL INDIANAPOLIS GP

At far right: Valentino Rossi, middle, has the top spot on the podium after winning the 2008 Red Bull Indianapolis GP. With him are Nicky Hayden, left, who came in second, and Jorge Lorenzo, third.

Motorcyclists do some practicing in the rain in preparation for the inaugural Red Bull Indianapolis GP event. After a 99-year absence, Red Bull Indianapolis GP riders don't let rain interfere with their track time.

American Nicky Hayden leads Valentino Rossi in the early going of the Red Bull Indianapolis GP race in 2008. Rossi will be ahead with eight laps to go when rain and high winds force a halt.

Bernie Ecclestone, the boss of Formula One, in the garage area of the Speedway in 2004. *Dick Mittman collection*

The Speedway signals the beginning of the Formula One era in 2000. That's the Hall of Fame Museum in the background, with the downtown Indianapolis skyline five miles farther east.

# U.S. GRAND PRIX FORMULA ONE AT INDY

Why would little-known Formula One driver Zsolt Baumgartner get a ride on his teammate's shoulders after the 2004 race at the Speedway? By finishing eighth, he had just scored the one and only point of his entire F1 career. More importantly, it assured Minardi of not having to pay its own expenses in '05. *Dick Mittman collection*

Above: International flags, banners and a red Ferrari pulling out of the pits signal the arrival of Formula One at Indy. *Dick Mittman collection*

Below: The Speedway's main stretch received an extreme makeover in 1999-2000 to accommodate the United States Grand Prix.

**Tony George.**

If we can get the timing and spacing where we need it to be, it's my goal to have four world-class events at the Speedway every year. Based on the experience we've had, I'm confident we can handle it. — Indianapolis Motor Speedway CEO Tony George

**Dominating the Speedway skyline, this 153-foot-tall galvanized steel and glass tower borrows iconography from the "pagodas" of ancient history and from the minimalist tower in use from the late '50s through the '90s. At sunrise, the Pagoda is a graceful work of art.**

CHAPTER 15

# A 100TH BIRTHDAY FACELIFT

At the turn of the 20th Century, this big white barn along Little Eagle Creek north of the Crawfordsville Pike anchored a farmyard. Now, it's the main feature at the 18th hole of the Brickyard Crossing Golf Course.

One thing Carl Fisher and the boys weren't too much worried about when they planted their race track in the boonies west of Indianapolis 100 years ago was its impact on the neighborhood. There wasn't one.

You had the Ben Hur interurban waiting station and a half dozen farms along the Georgetown Pike. And that was about it.

Carl could invite a few hundred thousand strangers to his place once a year without much ado from his neighbors because they were few and far between. Besides, they were invited, too, and they quickly learned it would be both lucrative and soon over.

That's changed in recent years, at least in part because more big events at the track have altered the rhythm of life in town. True, the 500 took the better part of a month to play out, but people knew for sure it would soon end by June 1.

With events like the Allstate 400 at the Brickyard and Formula One and now the motorcycle races coming to Indy, the crowds, the traffic and the economic impact are all bigger. What was once just an intense spring fling for Speedway townspeople has turned into an on-again, off-again relationship that now lasts until fall, and it has sparked a lot of conversation about how the town and the track might relate to each other in the years ahead.

As Tony George looks to the Speedway's next 100 years, he sees a far different landscape than Carl Fisher did in 1909 or his grandfather did in 1945. It's an urban scene any way you turn.

The Town of Speedway didn't exist in 1909. Today, as one of three autonomous municipalities completely surrounded by the city of Indianapolis,

**Joie Chitwood.**

Isn't it amazing after 100 years that we're the only sports property I know of that has elevated its community to international recognition? When you travel around the globe and you tell people you're from Indianapolis or Indiana, the comeback is, 'Racing, right? Racing, racing.' As Hoosiers, it's in our DNA. Indy is racing." — Indianapolis Motor Speedway President and COO Joie Chitwood

**Except for about 1,000 feet outside the backstretch, the entire track is encircled with grandstands on race day in 2001.**

it is home to 12,500 people.

Sixty years ago, it was the ideal post-war suburb, a great place to set up housekeeping, raise a family, and live as normally as you could expect to in the shadow of two mammoth edifices on the edge of town: the Speedway and the Allison Division of General Motors. But with the growth of more upscale communities farther west, fewer families have been staying put. Home ownership is down, as is overall population.

Meanwhile, by almost any measure, the track is enjoying a renaissance with the Red Bull Indianapolis GP bike races and other events.

Economic impact studies are a bit of a black art, but experts agree the Indy 500 and the Allstate 400 at the Brickyard together inject hundreds of millions into the local economy every year. Price tags for the never-ending capital improvement projects at the track are seldom revealed.

Today, the place sparkles. Tony George thinks his grandfather would approve.

So that's the backdrop as the 100th birthday of the Racing Capital of the World prompts the rhetorical question: What's next?

**Wheelchair racers cross the famed Speedway "Yard of Bricks" during the OneAmerica 500 Festival mini-marathon.**

**Among the many charity events for which the Speedway plays host to annually, one of Chairman of the Board Mari Hulman George's favorites is The Humane Society's "Mutt Strut" to benefit dog rescue. That's race driver Sarah Fisher with her Aunt Barb's pet Dalmatian.**

**A river of humanity flowing north on Georgetown Road becomes a torrent within minutes of the end of the 2008 500.**

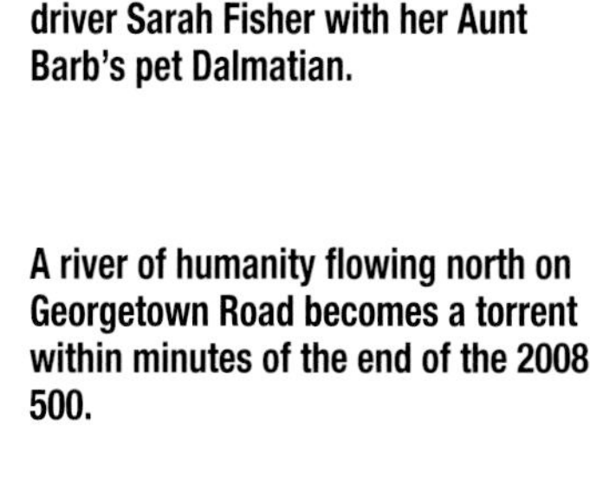

With the town and the track seemingly on opposite trajectories, can the crossing point become a doorway into a future not even Carl Fisher would have envisioned?

Don't bother looking long term. If such a thing as an automobile is still around 100 years from now, will people still race it? Who knows. But people *are* looking five or 10 years out, and what they're seeing is maybe more exciting than anything the track and the town have experienced since those days in 1909 when Carl Fisher's dream was taking shape. Or in '45, when Tony Hulman kept it alive.

The big picture is already defined. Dubbed Speed Zone, it's the work of the Speedway Redevelopment Commission. The plan comprehends the most extensive makeover of the area since 1909. It would change the face of the track and the character of the area.

Scott Harris, executive director of the commission, says the goal is to re-invigorate his town. Creating open space around the track is

**Almost 100 years old and counting, these original bricks look none the worse for wear.**

**Every time it is resurfaced, the track gets a new "Yard of Bricks." If a brick can't be reused, it is replaced from a stash of original 1909s.**

one goal. Paving the way for a variety of themed retail and entertainment projects in the town's business district is another.

"The idea," he says, "Is to reinforce the obvious—that this truly is "The World Capital of Racing."

Phase one would shift 16th Street south, away from the track, and create a large green zone with room for a hotel and other large structures. For the first time, passersby will get a proper look from a distance at the track's great south face.

The plan would also close Georgetown Road and create a mile-long linear park along the west side of the track. Suddenly, the hemmed-in Speedway pictured so often from above on race day would have a spectacular open border. Assuming minimum glitches, the transformation should be complete by the 100th anniversary of the first 500 in 2011.

In needs to be said that projects like this have been proposed before. There was one in the '50s involving a monorail, which would have linked key spots inside the track with depots outside. There was another for a Disneyesque theme park. They never got off the ground.

This one is different, if for no other reason than both Tony George and Joie Chitwood like it. They see it dovetailing nicely with their vision of the track's immediate future.

"We're not Disney," Tony says. "There's a unique connection between the track and the town. Clearly, much of the business here is related to racing. We expect to continue to be a part to the town's future vitality."

As the Speedway's president, Joie is Tony's second-in-command. His grandfather raced here. He is steeped in the track's history and traditions, and he thinks the plan keeps the faith.

"This is a very aggressive undertaking," he says. "It's in keeping with our efforts to enhance an already world-class racing venue. And it's a step in the right direction for a town that needs some economic development."

Like an exuberant teen-ager on a growth spurt, the Speedway of the 21st century is in a constant state of change. It's more than a physical thing.

**When looking back upon Tony George's leadership, IMS historians will likely save their highest praise for his leadership in the energy-absorbing barrier revolution. It began in 1998 when IMS and the Indy Racing League funded the PEDS barrier (Polyethelene Energy Dissipating System). With the research and development muscle of the University of Nebraska, the IMS and IRL led the way in the development of the SAFER barrier (Steel and Foam Energy Reduction) starting in late 1998, with its worldwide debut at IMS in May 2002. NASCAR joined the effort in September 2000. Most oval speedways more than a mile in length, including every oval that hosts IndyCar Series or NASCAR Sprint Cup events, have since installed the system.**

The PEDS barrier in 1998.

The second-generation SAFER barrier, 2005.

Art and Kathy Koch haven't missed a 500 since 1960. Here they and their family attend one together. Grandson Camden is next to Art, Kristen and Matt Wade are to Kathy's left; behind them are Chris Miller and Karan Koch. Kathy Koch: "For me, this is the only place in the world to be today."

It's cultural. To remain the world's premier motor sports entertainment venue, the Hulman/George family knows the facility must continue to offer an unmatched customer experience.

"But everybody's trying to do that," says Chitwood. "I hope what distinguishes us is our traditions, our facility, our concern for our customers, and the balance we try to bring to the commercial side of the sport.

"We've all been in situations where commercialism got in the way. But at Indianapolis, we vow to keep offering great sporting events in a clutter-free environment with our participants, our fans and our sponsors all knowing by how we treat them that they're truly special to us," he says.

"We vow to maintain an environment for our traditions to flourish, but we're not going to invent any.

"I think it's great that, on his own, Louis Meyer drank buttermilk in victory lane in 1936. I think it's great that, on their own, Dale Jarrett and Todd Parrott decided to kiss the bricks in '96.

"And we vow not to tamper with the pre-race ritual at the 500.

"From taps to the blessing to Florence Henderson and Jim Nabors singing, to the fly-over to the National Anthem to Mari giving the command to start your engines, there's no better 30 minutes in motor sport."

Standing up in the saddle is routine for this lead rider on the Indianapolis Metropolitan Police Department's motorcycle drill team.

A perfectly synchronized fly-over is when the planes arrive the moment the last note of the National Anthem is sung.

The Purdue University band catches a breather between pre-race exercises.

**Tony Hulman.**

In 1987, there's no more space on the original Borg-Warner Trophy for the sculptured likeness of the winning driver, so it is mounted on a base with room for more bas-relief images. The first likeness on the new base is in gold. It's of Tony Hulman. Today, it remains the only likeness of a non-winning driver anywhere on the trophy.

# Bibliography

Indiana Book of Records.

*Indy 500 Pace Cars,* Auto Editors, Consumer Guide, 1998.

*Story of Speedway, The,* Speedway Civic Committee, 1976.

Binford, Tom. *A Checkered Past: My 20 Years As Indy 500 Chief Steward*, Cornerstone Press, Chicago, 1993.

Bloemker, Al. *500 Miles To Go: The Story of the Indianapolis Motor Speedway*, Frederick Muller Ltd., England, 1961.

Bodenhamer, Donald J., and Barrows, Robert G. *The Encyclopedia of Indianapolis*, Indiana University Press, 1994.

Borgeson, Griffith. *The Golden Age of the American Racing Car*, SAE International, 1997.

Burns, John M. *Thunder at Sunrise: A History of the Vanderbilt Cup, the Grand Prize and the Indianapolis 500, 1904-1916*, McFarland & Company, 2006.

Carnegie, Tom. *Indy 500: More Than a Race*, McGraw-Hill, New York, 1987.

Cathcart, Charlotte. *Indianapolis From Our Old Corner*, Indiana Historical Society, 1965.

Davidson, Donald, and Shaffer, Rick. *Autocourse Official Illustrated History of the Indianapolis 500*, Crash Media Group, 2006.

Fisher, Jerry M. *Pacesetter: The Untold Story of Carl G. Fisher*, Comp-Type Pub, 1998.

Foster, Mark S. *Castles in the Sand: The Life and Times of Carl Graham Fisher* (Florida History and Culture), University Press of Florida, 2000.

Fox, Jack. *The Illustrated History of the Indianapolis 500*, 1994.

Huntington, Roger. *Design and Development of the Indy Car*, HP Books, 1981.

Lewis, W. David. *Eddie Rickenbacker: An American Hero in the Twentieth Century*, The John Hopkins University Press, 2008.

Madison, James H. *Indiana Through Tradition & Change: A History of the Hoosier State & Its People, 1920-1945*, Indiana Historical Society, 1982.

McDonald, John. *Lost Indianapolis* (Images of America), Arcadia Publishing, 2002.

Routte. Jane Carroll. *Speedway* (Images of America), Arcadia Publishing, 2004.

Scott, D. Bruce. *Indy: Racing Before the 500*, Indiana Reflections LCC, 2005.

Shaw, Wilbur. *Gentlemen, Start Your Engines: An Informal Autobiography of an Immortal Racing Driver, Sportsman and Gentleman*, Coward, McCann, 1955.

Rich, Taylor. *Indy Seventy-Five Years of Racing's Greatest Spectacle*, St. Martin's Press, 1991.

# INDEX

*Denotes a reference in a photograph and/or caption.